Michael Rebeiro leads a team of technology practice at an international law firm. Prior to embarking on his legal career he studied for the priesthood and spent a year as a voluntary worker in Nicaragua. He is an active member of the faith community at The Most Holy Trinity Church in Bermondsey, where he leads the Journey in Faith programme. He lives in London with his wife and two children.

FOR WINNING PRIZE
C'WORD (UNIVERSE '18)

Signs Given That We Might Act

Reflections on the Gospel of John

Michael Rebeiro

Book Guild Publishing

Sussex, England

First published in Great Britain in 2013 by
The Book Guild Ltd
Pavilion View
19 New Road
Brighton, BN1 1UF

Typesetting in Garamond by
YHT Ltd, London

Printed and bound in Great Britain by
CPI Group (UK) Ltd, Croydon, CR0 4YY

A catalogue record for this book is available from
The British Library.

ISBN 978 1 84624 875 7

To my wife and children – the greatest signs and wonders of God's love

Contents

Foreword

There is a huge hunger for the Word of God and an even greater hunger for material that will help us in a truly human way to open up the mysteries of the Divine. Deep theological tomes are for the few but when good words give us insight and help us make holy the lives we lead we have a find indeed. The Word has definitely found flesh in Mike Rebeiro's writing. Here is a book that time after time shines a light on those things that we try to live every day.

While in no way a biography of Mike's own spiritual development, his personal journey has given him, through some great ups and some big downs, the ability to let the Word speak. From an enthusiastic young man who wanted a relationship with God, via testing of vocation to responding to need in Nicaragua, to becoming a lawyer and celebrating the challenges and joys of family life, Mike has always put God in Jesus at the heart of who he is, whether he has felt at the heart of the church or sometimes on the outside looking in. His journey has given him an assurance that God is always there no matter what.

I see this book as a very useful tool in our journey of faith and even more useful as we are about to begin our Year of Faith. Let the strength of John's Gospel shine through the words that Mike shares with us, whether it is read as short meditations, a pilgrim's retreat, or just by someone who wants to hear a story. I feel that these seven signs will be not just seven insights but, as scripture says, and I paraphrase the words of Matthew, 'seventy-seven moments of grace'.

When we let the words of the Gospels touch our lives we are transformed. I am encouraged by the way the Gospels have spoken to Mike. I am also very happy that the odd sermon or two has added to his insight!

Rev. Canon Alan McLean

Acknowledgements

In writing this book I am grateful for the patience of my colleagues, especially those who have had to suffer my latest thoughts and commentary while travelling with me. I am also particularly grateful to Alan and Louise for their helpful comments and to my colleague Jane for her work in correcting my many errors and split infinitives.

Finally, my thanks go to my ever-suffering wife and my two children: you are the signs of God's love made real to me every day.

Signs and Wonders on the Journey

This book finds its genesis in a journey. It is the journey on which the beloved disciple invites us to accompany him as we witness the first part of the story of Jesus, the anointed one, the Christ. It is a journey in which we see the seven wonders and signs that Jesus performs. However, as we observe these signs we find ourselves being called on to be more than mere spectators of the events which took place some two thousand years ago. Today we are invited to accompany Jesus as we witness those signs take on new relevance for us, both individually and as the community of the Church. In the same way that those signs transformed the lives of those who witnessed them in Judea, if we are prepared to open our hearts to the power of the gospel, those same signs can have a transformational effect on us.

The right place to start any journey is, surprisingly, not at its beginning but in the steps that lead to the journey being undertaken in the first place – a fact that is equally true when it comes to this book. It is important for the reader to understand not only how this book came about, but also something of its author. To understand, interpret and judge any work, we must first seek to understand its origins and the particular perspective held by its writer.

I am a husband, a father to two young children and the

second son of first-generation immigrants from India, brought up in a staunchly traditional Catholic family. The story of my forebears has been one of travelling, leaving India in expectation and hope for a new land and a new home where a better life was promised.

I was born in 1964, a time of new beginnings for my family, but also a time of new beginnings for the Church as it came to grips with the meaning and consequences of Vatican II. I have two particular happy memories of early childhood which I now realise shaped much of my future life and my view of the Church. The first is of regularly attending Mass with my father at the age of around three. While I cannot remember the specifics of those events, I can still vividly recall the colours, sounds and smells of the liturgy, of the creed being intoned in Latin, and of incense rising to what I then thought was heaven, but was in fact the church roof. Overawed by this early experience of the liturgy, it was perhaps not surprising that, when I was old enough, I became an altar server and subsequently a member of the church choir.

My second memory is of visits from my great-uncle Cyril, a Jesuit priest who, although born in India, had been ordained for the priesthood in Lauvain, Belgium in 1937. He arrived in London a decade after my mother's family had migrated from Calcutta to London in the early 1950s. His visits were joyous occasions when my brother and I would happily play with our great-uncle, whom I fondly remember as a kind and gentle man with a generous and loving spirit. During his visits we would gather around our family table to eat a meal of Indian and English heritage and to share the stories of the coming into being of our own Anglo-Indian community and our family.

Perhaps it was this early comfort and familiarity with the

Church and the ordained ministry that in part led me to train for the diocesan priesthood many years later, in 1984. My decision to apply to the seminary was also due to a defining moment of faith in my life at the age of sixteen. It was then that I first realised that I had, actively and consciously, either to embrace and live out as an adult the faith passed down to me from my parents, or to let that faith go as a remnant of childhood. Yet, on reflection, my desire to enter the seminary was not born out of a real conviction that I had to be a priest, but rather that I felt a call to serve. Nevertheless, this call to serve confused not only me but also those around me. While my father was overjoyed at the thought of a priest within the family, my mother was overcome with sadness at the thought of grandchildren she would not have.

My confusion was there for all to see, although many people offered kind and in some cases humorous words of comfort. At the age of eighteen I was lucky enough to meet Pope John Paul II in Rome. Full of nerves and uncertainty as His Holiness approached me, in a moment of panic I asked his secretary what I should say. He kindly responded, 'Just don't tell him you're after his job!'

And so I entered the seminary, not knowing really what it was that God was calling me to, but with the firm intention that my vocation should be tested. It was not long before I realised that this was a test I would fail. Eighteen months later, with mixed feelings of both sadness and excitement at what might lie ahead, I left the seminary to start a career in law – a career I still find myself pursuing over twenty-five years later.

On my own faith journey since then I have had moments when I have been deeply attached to and involved in the community of the Church, yet there have been other –

often prolonged – times when I have felt estranged from the Church and attended Mass infrequently, if at all, although I have never lost or questioned my belief in God. Both of these extremes have been essential parts of my sometimes rocky faith experience, and I have encountered the risen Jesus both inside and outside the community of the Church.

It is perhaps unsurprising, then, that this book found its origin during the course of many journeys. In the last few years my job has increasingly demanded that I travel to different parts of the world. Not a month seems to go by when I am not boarding a flight or catching a train, as the demands of a global economy and an internationalised workforce find me visiting colleagues and clients throughout the world. In the last three years I have travelled from Europe to the Middle East, from the Americas to Australia, and from Africa to Asia.

As I began to write these words, I found myself sitting in a hotel lobby in Johannesburg waiting to catch a flight back to London. As I now complete them, I find myself sitting on the evening Amtrak train from Penn Station in New York to Back Bay in Boston. Tomorrow I will fly to San Francisco before I finally make my way home to my family in London next week via Toronto and Montreal.

I am particularly fond of train journeys. They give me time to think, time to reflect and time to just sit back and watch the world pass by. I have also discovered that train journeys can take you to unexpected destinations. It was on a train journey some twelve years ago, while travelling to the baptism of a friend's son in Salisbury, that I discovered how our actual points of destination may be to places that we have not yet known or intended to visit. It was on that journey that I shared my unhappiness at the then state of my life with a close friend. I had known Alan, who was also a priest, from my early youth. Indeed he had been, and continues to be, a formative element in my faith experience.

As we sat in our carriage, after listening to me for some time, Alan began gently to persuade me to return to the Church after a nearly fifteen-year gap. A year later, it was in his parish, my newly adopted community, that I met Judith. In that same parish community we were married and, some four years later, our two children were baptised and welcomed into the family of God. And it is in that community that I now have the joy and privilege of sharing the faith journey of so many of the elect and candidates as they travel to their encounter to meet and know Jesus through the Rite of Christian Adult Initiation.

Little did I know, as I boarded the train at London Waterloo for the relatively short ride to Salisbury some twelve years ago, that in so doing my life would take an unexpected yet joyful change of direction. Accordingly, I have since come to cherish all trips as potential expeditions of discovery: while I may have one destination in mind, I never truly know where the Lord will take me.

Tonight, the train is full of city commuters making the three-and-a-half-hour journey home to their loved ones in Boston. While this is a long daily commute by any standards, I still find myself feeling envious as I think of my own young son and daughter lying fast asleep in their beds in London. I also feel guilty as a father who cannot find enough time to spend with them and who is constantly dragged away on business. I hope and pray that as they get older they will understand the necessity of my long periods away from home.

I have taken this journey before, and on that occasion it

was during daylight hours. So I know it to be, in the light of the sun, a particularly pretty and picturesque route to take. The train in places travels through the most beautiful countryside and, in others, hugs the rugged coastline looking out to the ocean. Tonight, however, we travel in semi-darkness. The Amtrak rocks from side to side at high speed down a winding track, weaving its way through barely lit New England communities covered in the white winter snow of New York State and Massachusetts.

It occurs to me that as a metaphor for our lives this particular journey is highly relevant. Sometimes we journey through the most breathtaking and remarkable places where it would be wonderful to stay and dwell for a while. On other occasions we are in the dark and do not really know where we are, let alone where our final destination will be. And sometimes life rocks us with such force that we feel that we will never recover. Yet we all live in certain hope that we will reach our final destination in peace and safety.

This evening I am travelling not alone but with colleagues from London, the Middle East and Australia. As we sit chatting, another colleague from Hong Kong has already gone ahead of us on the evening flight to San Francisco. These colleagues all started out as just that, colleagues, but as we have travelled together and shared our own stories along the way, we have become more to each other and are now firm friends. We share a common sense of purpose, a common sense of values and, most importantly, a common sense of humour, which is essential if we are to survive with sanity the business trips that we make. Having good companions on our journeys is vital. It is a lonely road that is walked alone.

On reflection, I have been incredibly blessed and lucky

on my travels. I have had the honour to meet new friends from many different countries and cultures. In so doing, many of the barriers of my own prejudices and pre-conceptions have been broken down. Closer to home, I have also had the blessing of sharing in the journeys of many in my own parish community in Bermondsey as we have walked together on a shared pilgrimage in faith, hope and love. Together, through the celebration of the Word of God proclaimed and at the table of the Eucharist, we have partaken in the intimate relationship that God calls us to share with him and with each other.

Through that voyage of discovery we have shared and celebrated our diversity, our deepest hopes and desires, our deepest worries and doubts. We have walked together hand in hand, discovering and growing deeper in our relationship with Jesus. I have been amazed by the honesty and courage of all of us as we have decided to take this 'road less travelled',[1] and as we have opened ourselves up to intimacy with each other and with God in the community of love we have come to share.

Wherever I have met new friends, either away from or at home, I have come to realise that, whether we are children of the great Abrahamic faiths of Christianity, Islam or Judaism, or belong to the mystical faiths of the East or, indeed, are of no faith at all, there will always be much more which draws us together than can ever pull us apart. As a fundamental and enduring truth there is a goodness and generosity of spirit at the heart of all people. Nevertheless, this truth continues to surprise me. Logically it should not, as that innate goodness and generosity, indwelling in the heart of each of us, finds its source in the

---

[1] M. Scott Peck, *The Road Less Travelled* (Arrow Books, 1990).

indwelling Spirit of the God who loves unconditionally and who has made and loved each of us into being. I was delighted to learn on a recent trip to Munich that the traditional Bavarian greeting '*Gruss Gott*' that I had heard on so many occasions and mistakenly thought meant 'How are you?' literally means 'I greet God in you'.

I have also discovered that the greatest joy of travelling is to return home to meet again with the three closest and most loving friends in my life – my wife, my daughter and my son. The uncontained excitement of our children as they hear my key turn in the lock of the front door always fills me with a joy beyond all telling. I am reminded of the words of the psalmist: 'Your children round your table like shoots of an olive tree.'[2] It is at these moments, in the utter delight of familial friendship and love, that I have also begun to glimpse something of the ever-accepting and unconditional hand of love and friendship that God holds out to each of us.

On my travels I have also rediscovered an old and yet surprisingly new friend, the Gospel of the blessed disciple John. Upon reflection, I have to say that like so many friendships, ours did not start out so well.

In my childhood I always found reading or listening to the Gospel of John difficult. Unlike the three Synoptic Gospels, the words of John appeared to me to be impenetrable, full of a theological language which was beyond my limited capacity to understand. In parts, the Gospel appeared to be long and unnecessarily wordy; it lacked the conciseness and brevity of, say, the Gospel of Mark.

---

[2] Psalm 128:3.

As a young altar server, tasked with carrying a heavy brass acolyte and standing in front of the priest as he read the Good News each Sunday, I would dread the length and density of the Gospel of John. The acolyte would grow heavier by the word and my arms and shoulders would correspondingly ache with increasing pain as each second passed slowly by. My one fear was that I would drop the acolyte and set fire to the cloth draped over the lectern from which the priest was reading. I would similarly fear the use of the lengthy fourth Eucharistic prayer, as the instruction to kneel with upright back while holding a torch by the side of the altar would always leave me with sore knees. In my opinion, the blessed disciple and the Church Fathers who had coined the fourth Eucharistic prayer had both had little regard for what their lack of brevity would mean for me and my fellow servers.

Then, at the age of sixteen, I attended a week-long retreat organised by the De La Salle community at St Cassian's Centre in Kintbury. I had been lucky enough to attend St Joseph's College, a De La Salle School in Beulah Hill, South London. The De La Salle brothers were an order founded by John Baptiste De La Salle in the latter part of the seventeenth century and they were, as they are now, dedicated to working with young people. In the 1970s, notwithstanding the fact that St Joseph's had lost first its independent and then its grammar school status, it was still regarded as one of the best state schools in South London where Catholic parents could send their sons.

The De La Salle brothers ensured that their pupils achieved results through a philosophy built upon hard work, faith and discipline. Even the smallest details had to be observed as the backbone of this method steeped in tradition. For example, from our first days we were taught that at the top of the left-hand margin of every piece of work that we completed, the letters JMJ should be inscribed to signify and remind us that all our work was to be offered up to Jesus, Mary and Joseph. Likewise, when we received our end-of-term report card from the headmaster it was forbidden to receive it with your left hand. Pupils who forgot this rubric would find themselves at best in detention or, at worst, with bruised knuckles. Individuality was certainly a value to be prized, but only after the virtues of conformity had been fully embraced.

The retreat centre at Kintbury, however, operated along very different lines. In the fresh and enthusiastic post-conciliar years it was run by a mixture of young lay people and brothers, with a freedom of the spirit designed to allow teenagers to discover their own innate value and worth. The central tenet upon which all flowed was best encapsulated by a sign which hung over the bar in the common room: 'God does not make rubbish, he just collects it.' As Rowan Williams wrote in similar terms of the spirituality of the Desert Fathers, this was not the expression of some sort of 'I'm OK you're OK method'.[3] No, the value and worth expounded at Kintbury were based on the simple premise that we are all the created sons and daughters of a loving Father and the adopted brothers and sisters of his loving Son Jesus.

I wish I could say that my desire to give up a week of what I considered to be my precious summer holidays was born out of a pious calling or desire to come to know God better. In all truth, however, it was prompted more by a desire to meet girls. For a young man attending a single-sex

[3] Rowan Williams, *Silence and Honey Cakes – The Wisdom of the Desert* (Lion Hudson, 2003).

Catholic school, this was a rare opportunity which was not to be missed.

The retreat was led by Brother Damian Lundy. Brother Damian was one of the most charismatic men I had ever encountered. Many will know him as editor of *Songs of the Spirit*[4] and the writer of many songs, including 'Song for a Young Prophet', but Damian also had a unique ministry to the young. Although he was in his forties then, he certainly had a youthful spirit which enabled him to empathise and reach out to the young people to whom he was called to minister. At that point in his life Damian was quite a large man. Although subsequent illness would reduce him to a shadow of his former self, I still remember him almost bouncing around the common room in Kintbury, filled with lively animation and passionate excitement, drawing us into the Gospel of John. At once I began to see past the dense language as we were literally dragged into the Gospel by Damian, who presented it not as dry and inaccessible theology, but as a thrilling story of the life and love of Jesus Christ. Damian told us that in the Gospel of John we would find a friend for life, although at that stage I did not understand the real truth of his words.

Later, under the pressures of school and studies, work and family life, as with so many friends from my youth, I lost touch. Nevertheless, God works in strange ways. It was not through excitement at the thought of meeting an old friend that I was drawn back to the Gospel of John, but through the boredom of a business trip. With nothing else left to read, I rediscovered a friendship which I hope will stay with me and challenge me for the rest of my life.

In that 'dead time' of waiting for trains to arrive or

---

[4] *Songs of the Spirit* (Kevin Mayhew Ltd, 1978).

planes to take off, travelling from one meeting or one country to another, I found myself growing ever more restless and bored. On such occasions, I would flick impatiently through business papers or local news journals, but I seemed to have lost any ability to concentrate on any one thing for any sustained period of time. At the same time, however, I sensed a nagging doubt that there was work yet to complete. On reflection, it should have come as no surprise to me that, since God is the Creator and exists outside time, he can take what I had improperly regarded as 'dead time' and use it in a new and creative way.

Nevertheless, at the time, I mistook this unease for a feeling that I had not prepared sufficiently for the next day's business meetings. So I found myself re-reading already familiar business papers in an effort to allay any fears that I may have had. Yet, even though I was always more than prepared for my meetings, I still had a feeling that there was in some sense unfinished business to attend to.

It was during one of these periods, while travelling on the last Eurostar train from Paris to London, that I found myself, out of bored desperation, reaching for a copy of the Jerusalem Bible and turning to the Gospel of John. As I began to read the Gospel I found myself once again being drawn into the narrative in a way that I had not experienced since those youthful summer days at Kintbury. I began to scribble down the thoughts, doubts and questions which the Gospel presented to me. And in those and later moments, the idea of this book began to take shape. Subsequent writings have taken place on the long flights to and from Singapore, en route to Hong Kong, New York or San Francisco. These reflections have literally been written on the move – in the spare moments of numerous journeys, on trains and planes, in hotel rooms and airport lounges.

As I have had the opportunity to reflect upon the words of John and, in particular, the seven signs which John describes, I have rediscovered, shouting out from the Gospel's pages, words which speak with direct relevance to our experience of faith and the world today. These words speak to us in the everyday routine of our lives, at work, at home or in the community in which we live and worship. They also speak to us as participants in the life of the Church as we travel together, as a pilgrim people, in search of the Lord. Perhaps it is fitting that this part of my own journey with John has been written, quite literally, while I have been on the move.

Whether the Gospel of John was written by the beloved disciple, or came from different sources has not been my concern. Others are much better placed to address these academic questions. Instead, what has been at the heart of my interest is what the words of John, and in particular the seven signs, say to us today. Although he is the only one of the Gospel writers to do so, it is right that John describes the miracles of Jesus as signs. Because that is what they are; they direct us on our journey. When we view these signs through the eyes of faith, we are directed to witness the loving and guiding hand of God directly intervening and working in our lives.

In the signs we also see John pulling us back to the wider narrative of God's relationship with the world and his chosen people, evidenced through the covenant and promise he has made. The history of this covenant finds its roots in the Old Testament and it should therefore come as no surprise that John also draws us back to the source of that narrative.

Through the seven signs, John invites us to take a journey which, if we accept, will prove to be transformational for each of us and hence transformational for the way we come together as Church and community in our parishes. If the constituent parts of the body are changed by the power of God, so the body itself can be transformed into a new and wonderful creation.

Thus in the wedding feast at Cana, we hear the voice of Jesus challenging us both individually and corporately (as the Church) as he asks, 'What do you want from me?' That question and our answer lie at the heart of our Christian response to the challenges of life.

After the joy and celebration of community at Cana, in the healing of the royal official's son we are asked to walk with the royal official on the lonely path of doubt and faith.

In the healing of the sick man at Bethesda, Jesus shakes us out of our comfortable lives by asking us to be people of the Sabbath. We are called to reach out to the nameless, unloved and alienated in our society. We are called to be truly radical in our approach and our witness.

As we witness the events of the feeding of the multitude, we are urged to live out and share with Jesus our threefold royal, prophetic and priestly baptismal mission. In so doing, we enter into a new Passover covenant with God.

As we sail with the disciples on the stormy sea to Capernaum, we witness their supranatural encounter with Jesus and learn a new meaning to our own intimate and sacramental encounter with Jesus in the Eucharist. In that encounter we are asked to fulfil our sacramental ministry by allowing our lives to be signs of Christ to all those we encounter daily.

As we stand by the blind young man, we too share in the suffering of the innocent. While we rejoice in his subsequent healing, we are asked to respond to the living Word of God and to be witnesses to the power of the healing Christ to an otherwise incredulous and increasingly violent world where God, for so many, is pushed to the margins. As we engage in that witness, our faith will grow in the furnace of aggressive opposition.

Finally, as we wait in the cold, dark, stench-filled tomb with Lazarus, we are called to new life by the voice of the Lord. We too are called to be signs of resurrection, offering new life to a world where for many the smell of death and the tomb has become a prison from which there is no escape. We are called to live out the great liberating and salvific mission of the Church.

In this light, our reading of the Gospel of John and the signs and wonders it contains will make us at times feel distinctly uncomfortable. This is no bad thing. The gospel is only good news if we allow it to work within us and transform us. We must be receptive to receiving and acting upon the Word of God. To paraphrase Brother Damian, the Word of the Lord must be deep within our spirit.[5]

That Word of the Lord will call and challenge us to new ways of living, thinking and loving in the power of Jesus Christ. For many of us, bound by the inherited restrictions of the secular world, this will be counterintuitive. Not only will it be contrary to our experience of the world and the communities in which we live, but it may also run against the comfortable experience of church which most of us have and which is contained in one hour on a Sunday morning.

Yet, in the Gospel of John, we truly witness signs recorded so that we may believe that Jesus is the Christ,

---

[5] Damian Lundy, 'Song for a Young Prophet' in *Songs of the Spirit* (1978).

the Son of God and that, believing this, we may have life through his name.[6] But equally, in that new life, the signs are given not only that we might believe, but that, like those early disciples of Jesus, we might also act.

[6] John 20:31.

1

'Woman, what do you want from me?'

The wedding feast at Cana (John 2:1–12)

Our journey starts at the beginning of Jesus' public ministry with the story of the wedding feast at Cana, a story familiar to us all. It is the first of the seven 'signs' that John, the beloved disciple,[1] tells us that Jesus performs in his ministry.

In our childhood, apart from the nativity narrative, it might be one of the first stories we learn about Jesus. Perhaps this is not surprising, for it is something that children can readily understand. It begins to instil within us a sense of awe of Jesus. He is seen as the wonder-worker, a great magician who can miraculously turn water into wine. Thus, through the sign at Cana, our infant faith begins to grow and we begin to believe in Jesus as more

---

[1] Authorship of the Gospel is ascribed to the beloved disciple by certain commentators. See Richard Bauckham, *The Testimony of the Beloved Disciple* (Baker Academic, 2007). For a contrary view, see, among others, Raymond E. Brown, *The Gospels and Epistles of John*, 4th ed. (Liturgical Press, 1992).

than just a performer of parlour tricks, but rather as the Son of God.

Then, as we grow older and our faith develops further, we may begin to see other, more symbolic meanings in the sign, such as Jesus affirming the importance of marriage. After all, is it not striking that the first of Jesus' signs takes place at a wedding feast, in the centre of a family celebration? Much later in our journey, as our faith and understanding grow stronger still, we begin to see, perhaps, a more fundamental truth, the foretelling of our sacramental faith. As water is turned into wine and shared amongst all, so wine becomes for us the blood of Christ, shared and offered to all at our celebration of the Eucharist.

Yet our familiarity with the story can sometimes prevent us from exploring other more fundamental truths of this event in Jesus' life. Yes, on one level it is easy to see the story as nothing more than a 'miraculous' sign pointing to the divinity of Jesus. However, if we leave the story there we miss the opportunity to witness what Jesus is revealing to us today. If we are prepared to go further, to place ourselves into the Gospel story, we find that it is rich with imagery and meaning. In that richness, and at the beginning of our journey with Jesus, we will discover that he sets out a challenge. This challenge is made to each of us, both individually and collectively as the body of Christ, the Church. It is therefore no coincidence that this challenge is made in the setting of community and love.

Celebration interrupted

Of the moments in life when we come together to celebrate, perhaps one of the greatest is the celebration of marriage, precisely because it is a celebration of love. We come together as witnesses for two people as they administer this great sacrament of love to each other. And no matter how big or small the wedding may be, at the centre of the sacrament is the celebration of community, the celebration of a man and a woman bound together in the love of Christ. It is not surprising that St Paul used the image of Christ as husband of the Church, in a profound mystery bound together in the intimacy of love, the true perfection of community.[2]

We will all have fond memories of weddings during which we have been privileged to share in the joy of the bride and groom. But let us try and imagine ourselves as witnesses to the events of that day of love in Cana. We are at a busy and joyful wedding celebration. It is a hot summer's day and the guests have arrived, dressed in their finest clothes. Some have travelled a great distance to be here, to be part of the celebration of this couple's love. There is a definite air of anticipation and excitement.

The bride looks radiant and beautiful. In the midst of this celebration perhaps we chance upon her as she gazes on the bridegroom with a heart full of love. 'As an apple tree among the trees of the wood, so is my love among young men. In his delightful shade I sit, and his fruit is sweet to my taste.'[3] For his part, the groom looks adoringly at his new wife. He is filled with the pride of a newly married man and the thought that, out of all the men in Cana, she, this most beautiful and gentle of girls, has agreed to spend the rest of her life with him. 'As a lily among the thistles, so is my beloved among girls.'[4]

---

[2] Ephesians 5:23.
[3] The Song of Songs 2:3.
[4] The Song of Songs 2:2.

It is a moment of intense joy and happiness, one in which all have come to share. There is music, dancing and laughter. Months of preparation and planning by the bride's and bridegroom's families have gone into this day. The guests have been treated to the finest food. The wine is flowing, 'and your palate like sweet wine ... Flowing down the throat of my love, as it runs on the lips of those who sleep.'[5]

And then, quite unexpectedly, in the midst of the celebration, the wine runs out. The celebration is interrupted.

One cannot begin to imagine the chain of events that may have led to this dreadful happening. Has the bride's father simply underestimated his guests' capacity to drink, or have limited finances prevented him from buying the right amount of wine? Maybe it has been an unexpectedly hot day and the wine has been consumed all the quicker? Or, worse still, have the servants stolen or indeed drunk the wine themselves?

Remember, for a moment, the meticulous planning that went into the wedding celebrations you may have had within your own family. From the invitation, to the church, to the flowers, to the reception and the seating plan, nothing was left to chance. Indeed, I recall the almost military precision that went into the preparation and planning of my own wedding day. Imagine, then, how the bride and bridegroom and their families must feel on this special day as events turn out not at all as expected. Whatever the cause, it is a moment of great embarrassment for the families of the bride and bridegroom. What will their guests say? Surely they will never be able to live down this disgrace in Cana! This is not the start to their married

---

5 The Song of Songs 7:10.

life they had wanted or indeed imagined. How will they be able to live with the shame of what has happened? What they hoped would be an event forever remembered by the community as a celebration of joy and love will now be remembered for a very different reason.

Amongst the guests are a group of young men, drinking, laughing and enjoying the occasion. It is at this point that one of the female guests turns to one of these young men, her son, interrupting the group's revelry. She simply says, 'They have no wine.'[6] To a bystander this may appear to be a rude complaint from a meddlesome guest. To the son's friends it may be viewed as the son's mother interfering, causing the young man, not least, some degree of embarrassment. However, it is unlikely to be interpreted by many as a plea for help.

Yet the son's response shows us that there is something much more happening here. Mary does not bring an entreaty to Jesus; she does not express a desired outcome. She simply brings the situation to him and in so doing places him firmly in the 'now' of the event. The mother knows her son, as only a mother may, and knowing her son as she does, she speaks with expectation, she speaks with hope, she speaks with a voice of faith.

How does the son respond? Jesus turns to his mother and says, 'Woman, what do you want from me? My hour has not come yet.'[7] On first reading, this may seem merely like a mild rebuke to a mother by a son who has been interrupted from the festivities of the party. If we take Jesus' answer to Mary at the purely human level, it is perhaps understandable. A young man is at a party,

---

[6] John 2:3.
[7] John 2:4.

celebrating with friends, when his mother interrupts him, dragging him and his thoughts away from the celebration, embarrassing him. But, on another level, there may be a realisation that his hour has indeed now come: he must put away the things of his youth to begin the journey of his public ministry, a journey that will ultimately end in apparent despair, pain and death on the cross at Golgotha.

In considering Jesus' response, however, let us also reflect upon the role of Mary in the Gospel of the beloved disciple. In the Gospel Mary appears only twice, here at the wedding feast, at the beginning of Jesus' public ministry, and then again at the foot of the cross in the moments immediately before Jesus' death. At Cana, the first thing that surprises us is the way that Jesus refers to his mother. Ostensibly he does not address her with any of the affection you would expect from a son to his mother. Nor does he address her with a familial term, calling her 'woman' rather than 'mother'. Compare this with the tenderness of the cross where Jesus speaks of Mary, just moments before his death, as a 'beloved mother'.[8]

Commentators have argued that by calling Mary 'woman', Jesus is bringing to mind Eve. As Eve was the mother of humanity, so Mary becomes the mother of the new humanity, the new disciples of Jesus.[9] Certainly this would bring a wholeness to Mary's role within the Gospel of the beloved disciple. At Cana she is presented as the mother of all believers – as mother to the Church. At the cross her role is more intimate and she is given as a mother for each of us when Jesus says to the beloved disciple,

[8] John 19:25–27.
[9] See Brown, *The Gospel and Epistles of John*.

'"This is your mother!" And from that hour the disciple took her into his home.'[10]

On another level Jesus firmly shows that he now has to make a break with his mother and family. The new road he must take, ultimately to Golgotha, will be a painful and lonely one. And yet, as we shall see at Cana, Mary's role is not only integral to the sign, but it may also be argued that her role constitutes a greater sign for us today than the turning of water into wine.

But let us seek to go behind Jesus' seemingly impatient response and ponder the question that he poses. For this question is at the heart of the challenge of the Gospel and is presented to us at the very beginning of our journey. It is a question that Jesus asks each of us. It is also a question that Jesus asks us as the body of the Church. The question simply is, 'What do you want from me?'

Perhaps in posing this question Jesus provides a deeper insight into the nature of God, building upon that which John has already provided in the first chapter of his Gospel. Here is a God who is intimately bound to and involved in his creation. This is a God who has been calling to the whole of humanity from before the beginning of time; a God who, in the words of the prophet Jeremiah, has known each of us before we were formed in the womb.[11] This is a God who has been calling us and who, at the very beginning of Jesus' public ministry, almost as a precondition to it, now asks us, 'What do you want from me?' In this context we can perhaps understand the words of Jesus. And, in the impatience of a young son's response, we may also hear the urgency of a loving God, calling each

---

[10] John 19:27.
[11] Jeremiah 1:3.

of us, seeking to touch our hearts and challenge us to be recreated and transformed.

What do you want from me?

So here in the first sign we are met by the challenger God, calling to us, 'What do you want from me?' How do we respond to Jesus? Whatever our tradition, if we are truly to affirm ourselves as followers of Christ, Jesus' question demands a response. We must affirm what we want, what we yearn for, what we desire. Like Mary, do we truly want and desire to bring Jesus into the 'now' of the events of our lives to bring us new life? Our answer to that question will depend on the emotional and spiritual place in which we find ourselves when we hear the call of the Lord.

Sometimes our answer will come from a place of need. We may be lonely, in despair, in mourning or crying out for healing. Battered by the world around us, we are all in a desperate daily search for wholeness. Today, our pace of life places so many burdens and worries upon our shoulders. We worry about our job security. We worry about whether we can pay the bills each week. We worry about getting our children into the 'right' school. We worry for our children growing up in an increasingly violent society. We worry about the damage we are doing to our environment and climate. We allow ourselves to inhabit a frightening world, yet sometimes we may find ourselves worrying when life is going well because we feel that it cannot last for ever. We worry about worrying!

For some of us, it may be that our answer comes from a place of defiance and anger. We may be roaring in rage against the world. We may be angry with the circumstances of our lives, with our parents, with our partner, with our children. We may be holding on to old hurts which we have allowed to fester so long inside us that they have become loud, angry sores. Perhaps we are angry with the Church or its stewardship. We may feel that the Church has strayed from the path along which Christ would lead us. We may feel that its teachings are too harsh and that we, or those we hold dear, are excluded. We may feel that those in leadership have abused our trust. It is a sad fact that the clergy abuse scandal has, in certain cases, resulted in many leaving the Church. For example, in 2010 it was estimated that over 180,000 Catholics left the Church in Germany. Dominik Schwaderlapp, the Vicar General of Cologne, recognised that 'people are using Church departures as their personal form of protest and as a way to show their disgust with the scandal'.[12]

At other times we may witness the world around us, in all its pain and anguish, and even turn our anger on God. We may be like the impoverished King Lear wailing against the storm, crying, 'Blow, winds, and crack your cheeks; rage and blow.'[13] Like Lear, perhaps we too have a fool for our only company – save that for us the fool is our own ego and selfish desire. Often our anger may be caused by a realisation that the path we want to choose for ourselves is not the path that God wants us to walk with him.

The simple truth is that our deepest desires do not always accord with the plan of new life that the Lord has for each of us. It is unusual for many of us to recognise, accept and live this fundamental truth of our human existence. Rather, we seek to limit God's plans by our own

---

[12] Niels Sorrells, in the *National Catholic Reporter*, 12 April 2011, reporting on a study conducted by the German weekly newspaper *Die Zeit*.
[13] Shakespeare, *King Lear*, Act 3, Scene 2.

restricted and impaired vision. St Thérèse of Lisieux wrote, 'On this earth it is rare indeed to find souls who do not measure God's Omnipotence by their own narrow thoughts.'[14]

Consequently, at the level of the Church, perhaps our view of where the Church should be and what it should be teaching does not accord with the plan of life that the Lord has for the body of Christ. Do we have the courage to ask ourselves whether our desires are truly attuned to the values of God's Kingdom, much less than with the will of God? Do we have the courage to submit totally to the will of God and really believe that it is 'in him that we live, and move, and exist'?[15]

In the rush of our daily existence we convince ourselves that we can compartmentalise our faith, somehow building up barriers between our everyday lives and the call of life to which Jesus challenges us to respond. Yet in so doing we seek to diminish the very being and essence of God. It becomes easy for us to put God in a box that we get out and open for an hour each Sunday. It takes an act of true courage, and an act of true faith, to let God into every aspect of our lives, to let God out of the box, so we can pray like the poet John Donne:

> Batter my heart, three person'd God; for You
> As yet but knock, breathe, shine, and seek to mend;
> That I may rise, and stand, o'erthrow me, and bend
> Your force, to break, blow, burn and make me new.[16]

On other occasions we may find ourselves in a place of

---

[14] *Story of a Soul: The Autobiography of St Thérèse of Lisieux* (Christian Classics Ethereal Library, ccel.org).
[15] Acts 17:28.
[16] John Donne, *The Divine Poems*, 10.

celebration, just as at Cana, where we want nothing more than to share our happiness with our friends and loved ones. Possibly these are moments brought about by the birth of a child, the tenderness and discovery of new love, or the joy and affirmation of old friendships. These are instances of incredible joy and contentment, occasions of love and tenderness which even give us a glimpse of the promised joy of life and love eternal. In this place our only real response and desire is to rest in the delight of God and in the loving acceptance of our family or community.

More often than not, however, we simply do not know what we want of our God. We do not know how to respond to the question that Jesus poses. We are faced with a huge number of choices, of possible journeys to take, but we are left in a state of confusion and unknowing. The result is that we find ourselves living our lives frozen in a state of indecision. How do we make the right choice? Are we on the right path? Am I doing the right thing?

Today we seem to be obsessed by choice. Our politicians would weave a narrative which dictates that the greater the choice available to us, the greater our own personal prosperity and well-being will be. Our media- and product-driven society inundates us with choices we must make. And so we convince ourselves that we must pick the right car, the right brand of handbag, the right and very latest choice of television or mobile phone. We must live in the right part of town and have the right sort of holiday. We order our lives around choice. We must have the right to choose! Choice becomes our new goal, a new obsession, our new right, and if we are not careful, our new god. Then, like the worship of all false idols, the worship and pursuit of choice will ultimately lead us away from our Lord. This overemphasis on choice is based on a principle

11

which puts the individual above the community. It always put my rights above those of my neighbours.

Through choice we are falsely led to believe that we can find emotional and spiritual freedom. However, the sheer weight of choices we are presented with can bear down upon and oppress us. We can become confused and feel the weight of a spiritual burden on our hearts. In our very pursuit of choice, we are faced with the danger of being unable to make the right choices. We know we are in need, but we do not know the answer to that need. Even if we think we know with our minds what we want, our hearts are in a state of constant turmoil. We can find ourselves in a state of inner conflict and that conflict, if not resolved, will ultimately damage us.

Anyone who has ever cared for small children will know that giving them unlimited choice will inevitably lead to pain and disaster. Children flit from one decision to another. My wife and I now know that as parents it is our role to protect our son and daughter from their inability to make truly informed choices. It is unhealthy to present a small child with too much choice. Their decisions, as they develop, must be guided and directed along the right paths so that, as they grow, they begin to feel a sense of certainty both in who they are and in the nature of the world around them.

On one occasion, as a reward for good behaviour, I took my daughter to a large department store with the promise that she could pick any doll she wanted. At first she ran from shelf to shelf in absolute excitement and joy at seeing so many wonderful dolls staring back at her, some dressed as princesses, others as various cartoon heroines. There were dolls of all sizes, colours and shapes. However, I noticed that her initial happiness soon turned into a state of anxiety. As she moved from one doll to the next, picking it up then putting it down, she became more and more distressed. Finally, she could take it no more and collapsed in the middle of the shop floor, in floods of tears. I could not understand why she was so distraught and why this opportunity of father-daughter bonding had gone so badly wrong. When I asked her why she was so upset, she replied through her tears, 'There are just too many to choose from, I don't know which one to pick!' I learnt a valuable lesson that day about choice.

Children need, indeed love, boundaries. They give up – albeit sometimes kicking and screaming – their right of choice over all parts of their life, from what they wear to what they eat, because they trust, as only a child can, their parents' ability to make the right choices for them. It is only as they grow older and begin to develop their own sense of what is right and what is wrong, their own moral compass, that a loving parent should gradually cede to them more and more levels of responsibility and choice.

So it is with us and our relationship with God. We all need spiritual and emotional boundaries. The extent to which we will give up our right of choice, the extent to which we are prepared to submit to the unknown will of an unseen God, will depend upon how much we are prepared to trust in that God. It will depend upon the extent to which we are prepared to prayerfully commit, now, to the living prayer of Jesus that we recite every Sunday at our Eucharistic celebration: 'Your kingdom come, your will be done, on earth as in heaven.'[17]

Wherever we find ourselves on hearing Jesus' call, whether it be a place of need, defiance, anger, confusion

---

[17] Matthew 6:10.

or joy, the truth is that Jesus still calls to us, inviting us to respond to his question, 'What do you want from me?'

Mary's response – an act of faith

So how does Mary respond to Jesus? What is her choice? What can we learn from her? As a loving mother, her response comes from a heart of love and, because of such love, a place of complete and utter trust in her son Jesus. This is the same response of faith that she has lived out all her adult life and affirmed over thirty years earlier when she declared to the messenger of the Lord, 'You see before you the Lord's servant, let it happen to me as you have said.'[18] As Jesus grew in her womb, as she became the living ark of the new covenant, so her response of faith grew in her heart. Mary's response now comes from a life of loving, caring for and knowing Jesus and also from a position of knowing who she is and her role in God's unfolding plan. Her response comes from being completely open to God. Mary's total openness, allowing her mind, soul, spirit and body to be laid open to God, at his disposal, is predicated by the words of his messenger, 'do not be afraid.'[19]

Like Mary, our response demands a degree of self-honesty, looking at who we really are, the place where we find ourselves in this moment of our life. To achieve this we too must come before God as Mary did, stripped bare, being prepared to let go of the choices we can make. And in this intimacy, 'God alone will tell me who I really am, and he

---

[18] Luke 1:38.
[19] Luke 1:30.

will do so only in the lifelong process of bringing my thoughts and longings into his presence without fear and deception.'[20]

The key point here is that this ongoing process in our lives can be accepted without fear, for we know that Jesus accepts us as we are, with all of our indecision, confusion, anger and pain. Consequently, as we come before the awesome and yet intimate challenger God, in 'this dialogue we come to understand ourselves and we discover an answer to our heart's deepest questions'.[21]

If we find this thought difficult or even frightening to accept, it is perhaps because we judge God by our own limited capacity to accept and love ourselves. But the 'word of God in fact, is not inimical to us; it does not stifle our authentic desires, but rather illuminates them, purifies them and brings them to fulfilment'.[22]

It is only when we come to know, accept and love ourselves that we come to know, accept and love those around us. It is only then that we can begin to undertake the salvific and liberating mission of the Church.

Jesus asks of Mary, 'Woman, what do you want from me?'[23] Her reply comes from a place of total trust in her son, and as such it is completely undemanding of Jesus. She does not tell him what to do, she does not even ask him to help, she simply tells the servants, 'Do whatever he tells you.'[24] In so replying she submits her will entirely to the plan of her son. Her response is one of faith and trust,

---

[20] Rowan Williams, *Silence and Honey Cakes – The Wisdom of the Desert* (Lion Hudson 2003).
[21] Benedict XVI, *Verbum Domini – Post-synodal Apostolic Exhortation on the Word of God* (2010).
[22] Ibid.
[23] John 2:4.
[24] John 2:5.

and this faith and this trust inspire others not only to act but also, as we shall see, to make a change of direction.

Do whatever he tells you

Let us think for a moment about the servants she addresses. They are most likely already in a place of fear: the wine has run out and, whatever the cause, the master will surely blame them. Will they be punished? Will they be beaten, or will some worse fate befall them? Yet, on Mary's quiet instruction, 'Do whatever he tells you', they move from a place of fear almost immediately to a place of trust and consequent action. In the story of the wedding feast it is easy for us to overlook the magnitude of such action.

If we were to run out of wine today at any celebration, we would most likely simply pop to the shops to buy some more. In our 24/7 culture there is always a local shop open to ensure that we never run out of provisions.

My wife and I once planned a dinner party to celebrate the eve of the New Year. We mistakenly thought our preparations were impeccable. The children were asleep in their beds, the table was laid, the wine was flowing and the joint of beef was in the oven. It was with horror, then, that I discovered, only thirty minutes before we were due to sit down to our feast, that our two-year-old son had, unbeknown to us, turned the oven off. Our prized joint of beef was still uncooked. Luckily, even late into the night on New Year's Eve, I was able to rush to the shops to buy more wine. This I served to our guests with an apology to the effect that dinner would not actually be served until the next year!

But in Cana no such feat was possible. The action

demanded here was not as simple as popping out to the supermarket. The task which Jesus asks of the servants is immense.

The beloved disciple tells us that at Cana there were six stone jars, each holding 25-30 gallons of water. That is some 150-180 gallons in total. To convert this into an image we can understand today, it is the equivalent of over 900 bottles of wine. The servants' first task is to fill these jars with water. There would have been no running water on tap, no hosepipes, no easy way of completing this task. So the servants, on Jesus' instructions, would have had to fill these jars with water by hand. It was not just a matter of filling the jars. Rather it was a matter of the servants consciously choosing to stop their immediate duties without reference to or permission from either the bridegroom or the president of the feast.

By electing to interrupt their existing tasks they were in danger of further angering their master, of further neglecting the guests at the feast. Food ceases to be served, plates are not cleared away, guests are ignored. Instead their efforts are put into filling the six stone jars with water. This is an act of faith – an act of faith which in turn is inspired by Mary's response of faith to Jesus. Their faith demands of them a change in their direction, a change in what they are used to doing, a change in their perception of what now really matters.

To the rational observer such a course of action would defy all logic and could, even charitably, be described as nothing short of foolish. What is even more striking is that the servants carry out Jesus' instructions not because Jesus asks them to act, but because Mary, his mother, a woman of faith, asks them. Her quiet faith inspires the servants to act without fear and seemingly without reason, at the word of Jesus. The faith of one woman in her son lifts the servants out of a place of fear and, once out of that place of fear, they are emboldened to act on Jesus' command.

As the servants act, they become even more courageous and faithful themselves. Not only do they fill the jars with water, but at Jesus' instruction to 'Draw some out now and take it to the president of the feast',[25] they take the water from the jars directly to the president of the feast to taste. In their shoes we might, at the very least, have first tasted the water ourselves to be sure that we were not going to become the laughing stock of the feast. They, however, do not. They trust and believe that the water will be wine. They trust in the word and actions of Jesus. They trust because, through Mary's faith, they have come to believe in Jesus.

Perhaps here is the first lesson we learn from the sign at Cana, a lesson that is to be found in the nature of the sign itself. We perhaps assumed that the sign was the turning of the water into wine, but possibly the greatest sign at Cana was Mary's unqualified and selfless response of faith to Jesus. It is through that response that the seemingly greater physical sign becomes possible. Mary becomes the true sign. At Cana Jesus calls to each of us, 'What do you want from me?' In so doing he calls us, like Mary, to respond in faith and thus become signs of inspiring faith for the world.

Before we leave the narrative, let us remember the president of the feast. He has an important role to play in our story. The servants present him with the new wine. The beloved disciple tells us that he does not know what has preceded this simple act of handing him a cup of wine. Beneath the level of his existence a disaster has occurred:

---

[25] John 2:8.

the wine has run out. The servants, at the command of Mary, have followed the instructions of Jesus; acts of trust and faith have been followed by a miraculous sign. Yet, throughout all these events, the president has been unaware of this unfolding drama.

In the president's response, which is one of great thanks to the bridegroom, there is no connection, in his mind, with either Mary or Jesus. Instead he lavishes praise on the bridegroom: 'you have kept the best wine till now.'[26] In the president's response we learn a new truth about the life of faith to which Jesus calls us. Our acts of faith, like the acts of faith of Mary and the servants, are sometimes never noticed, let alone recognised as coming from us. Rather than the acts of faith themselves being brought to the fore, it is the fruits of such actions that are the most important and hence must take centre stage. It is not important that we say that 'Jesus did this', but rather that the 'this' actually happened.

This may not always sit easily with our flawed human nature. We like, indeed need, to be appreciated. And our need to be thanked comes out of a need to be reassured. In our lives we constantly seek out opportunities for personal praise. We want to demonstrate that we are the cause of good actions and deeds. Likewise, we can sometimes be as quick to disown actions which do not result in the right outcome. However, the beloved disciple shows us at the wedding feast at Cana that Jesus asks of us another way. Actions that are truly grounded in the authenticity of faith in Jesus Christ are to demand no recognition or gratitude. They are not to be self-serving. We are to find our joy and

---

[26] John 2:10.

19

thanks in the knowledge that a Kingdom-valued result has been achieved.

We could leave our story there, but to do so would be to neglect one final part of the sign. As we shall come to see on our journey, John's sense of timing is all important. And so we must ask: why did Jesus choose to perform the first sign at a wedding feast?

Celebration renewed

We might describe the events at Cana as a celebration interrupted. In fact the narrative of the sign is replete with interruptions. The feast is stopped when the wine runs out. Mary interrupts Jesus' revelry with his friends. The servants are interrupted from their tasks by the words of Mary. However, the story of Cana ends with the resumption of celebration. The first sign takes place at a very public celebration – a marriage feast. We associate with such celebrations a range of emotions: joy, happiness and excitement. At wedding celebrations we are reunited with old friends and family, for such celebrations are primarily about family. We have the joyful sense of families coming together and new families being created through the sacramental work of the bride and the groom. But also, perhaps, we experience a sadness and sense of loss for those close loved ones who could not join in the happy occasion, and a sense of bereavement for those of our family who have gone before us. I remember the utter joy at my own wedding and, as I first saw my wife enter the church, I was moved to tears of happiness. But I also remember the totally unexpected sense of sadness I felt as, gathered with my family, I was suddenly reminded of my grandmother who had died some twenty-five years earlier. A flood of memories of playing happily with her as a small child were suddenly brought forth in this moment of celebration.

In this familial community of love we are brought together to celebrate love. Jesus' first sign, then, takes place in the midst of such a celebration and in this way Jesus brings us to one of the central messages of the Gospel. In the same way that Jesus' first public sign, his first public action, takes place in a community of love and joy, so we must live our lives in and as a community. For it is in the intimacy of community that we not only find out who we really are, but come to know and touch the intimacy of God. Our action, our work, is quite simply to celebrate love. The Desert Fathers knew this and recognised that being in community, being connected to each other, was essential to their Christian life. Rowan Williams quotes St Anthony the Great as saying, 'Our life and death is with our neighbour. If we win our brother we win God, if we cause our brother to stumble we have sinned against Christ.'[27]

This is the primary goal of community and of us coming together as a Church. And it is in the community of the Church that we are called to live our Christian vocation.

Essential to the human sense of celebration is the sharing of food and drink. Indeed, the very act of sharing our nourishment together can have a transformative effect on us. As the Dominican Angel F. Méndez Montoya has noted:

> Eating not only brings about physiological or biological change; it is also a means of psychological, affective, and

---

[27] Rowan Williams, *Silence and Honey Cakes – The Wisdom of the Desert*.

even spiritual transformation. Eating and drinking certain products and substances triggers particular moods, enkindles various degrees of emotions, and awakens memories.[28]

The act of sharing food and wine with one another has the transformative effect of bringing and calling us into community. The act of consuming food and wine, itself an intimate act, calls us into intimacy with each other. Travelling by myself, on many business trips I have felt the isolation of eating alone in restaurants, the sense of being alienated from those around me who are in communal meals of friendship or family.

Even in our busy and challenging world we still cherish celebrations through the sharing of meals. It is almost as if our capacity to rejoice is part of our DNA. We come together to celebrate key moments of our lives, moments of growth and love, and even moments of pain and anguish. We celebrate the birth of a child and the coming together of a beloved couple in the commitment of married life. We even come together to celebrate death, when we cherish and rejoice in the life of a loved one who has passed away. In all these celebrations, shared food and drink have a central and defining role to play.

All these very real human events are tied into the supranatural sacramental celebrations of our faith community. Faith in Christ, by its very nature, leads us into community. No matter how spiritually devoted we may think we are, we cannot be a church of one. It is in community that we come together to celebrate. The most important of all these celebrations, through the communal

---

[28] Angel F. Méndez Montoya, *The Theology of Food: Eating and the Eucharist* (Wiley Blackwell, 2009).

sharing of bread and wine, is the celebration of our food of faith, the Eucharist. It is in the Eucharist that we find spiritual, emotional and physical nourishment. It is in the Eucharist that we witness Jesus' actions at work, that we celebrate his life in the community of love. And, as we shall see in the fifth sign, it is in the Eucharist that we have an intimate encounter with the risen Jesus, where we celebrate and once again enter into the redemptive action of Jesus through his death and resurrection. What better cause of celebration could there be?

At the heart of our celebration of the Eucharist we are invited to experience the pain, the sorrow, the joy and the happiness of our Christian journey, and in so doing we experience the living redemptive action of Jesus. Here we experience both the 'tear and the smile',[29] the joyous sharing of our bread of life and the sacrifice which lies at the heart of our faith and at the core of our Eucharist. Who could refuse an invitation to such a celebration?

Yet Mass attendance in Europe has fallen dramatically over the last few years and there are very few signs that this trend is being reversed. We may point to our secular society and argue that this is the cause of that decline. Shops and cinemas are now open on Sundays and children's sports activities compete with Sunday morning Mass times. However, while we can point the finger of blame away from ourselves, and find a myriad of convincing reasons why many of our parish communities are in decline, we must also ask ourselves whether those very same parishes are communities of celebration. Do we come together as family to celebrate Jesus, the wine of

---

[29] Khalil Gibran, *A Tear and a Smile* (1914).

new life? Or do we come together to 'do church' each Sunday and in some way get our duty out of the way?

Sadly, so often in our parish communities we do not find celebrations. We find that the liturgy, quite literally 'the work of the people', has become a habit or, worse still, a chore. Very often it is ill-prepared, rushed and without exultation. As at Cana, we have run out of the wine of celebration, but unlike at Cana, we have no sign to give us hope. We have resorted to living off a spiritual fast-food diet. We do not know what to do. We act as bystanders at the feast, with our cups empty, thirsting for the new wine of life. We lack the courage of Mary's petition and the faith of the servants to act. In our parish communities we need to recapture and relive the joy and delight of the celebration of the wedding feast at Cana, because it is in that joy and delight that we will find true nourishment. We must rediscover the joy of *agape*.

This is not simply a matter of what type of liturgy we prefer. Those who argue that one form of rite is better than another or should be used to the exclusion of the other are in danger of putting up artificial barriers within our family, forgoing the unity of community for the preferences of individuality. Again, one person's individual choice takes precedence over that of their neighbour. In so doing they are reducing the liturgy to a market, where consumer preferences rule. And, as is the case with all barriers, they separate rather than build up community. The world will look in at us and see division rather than love, separation rather than unity. This is hardly the celebration to which all will be drawn. And yet so many within our Christian community simply do not understand this basic truth. I sadly recall attending a dinner hosted by one bishop who was anxious to find out from those attending what they thought was wrong with the Church today. One lady was quick to respond that the Church's decline was due to a lack of incense and Latin.

What is the truth that the story of the wedding feast tells us? It is that we are called to celebrate the joy of love, the joy of Christ in our lives through the celebration of and in community. At the heart of our celebration must be the inclusive, welcoming celebration of our Eucharist – a celebration that helps us in the task of *winning our neighbour*. As the psalmist tells us:

> Praise God in his holy place,
> praise him in the heavenly vault of his power,
> praise him for his mighty deeds,
> praise him for all his greatness.
> Praise him with fanfare of trumpet,
> praise him with harp and lyre,
> praise him with tambourines and dancing,
> praise him with strings and pipes,
> praise him with the clamour of cymbals,
> praise him with triumphant cymbals.[30]

We need to remember the joy of our celebrations. Whether we praise God with tambourines and dance or praise him with strings and pipe, let us remember to praise God! Our celebration, our joy and our love should act as beacons of hope to a world broken by fear, loneliness and despair.

At Cana we witness Jesus performing the first sign in the midst of community celebration and fellowship. In so doing he clearly directs us to the vital, life-giving importance of community for our lives.

Yet the call to community is counterintuitive for many in the secular world. In the secular world the 'I' is placed at

---

[30] Psalm 150:1–5.

the height of importance over and above the life of community. In the face of true witness to the joy of Christian community, secular society would try to steer us and others down a different path. The temptation, in the face of cynicism and derision, may be to retreat from a witness to the joy of our faith, to retreat from being a Church of the Sabbath – which, as we shall see in the third sign, is a Church called to be truly radical in her witness of faith.

The secular world fights to stop us celebrating. Indeed, we live in a society where employees are no longer allowed to be a witness to their faith by wearing a cross, and where even the celebration of the nativity story is prohibited in many schools for fear of causing offence. We are cautioned against witnessing to our faith in case it upsets others. The Anglican Bishop of Rochester, Michael Nazir-Ali, has observed, 'Much of this has come about because of a "neutral" secularist approach which refuses to privilege any faith. In fact, secularism has its own agenda and it is certainly not neutral.'[31]

Secularism may have its own anti-faith agenda. There are 'traditional values and cultural expressions that more aggressive forms of secularism no longer value or even tolerate'.[32] But, as we shall see in the third sign, if we look around us we can quickly see that our secular world is crying out in need of true celebration. Take a look around you on any day and you will witness a society full of those alone, in despair and in need of hope – a world in need of a new joy and a new life-giving and affirming celebration.

---

[31] Bishop Michael Nazir-Ali, 'Extremism flourished as UK lost Christianity', *Daily Telegraph*, 6 January 2008.
[32] Speech of Pope Benedict XVI. Given on his arrival in the United Kingdom at Holyrood House, 16 September 2010. Contained in *Heart Speaks unto Heart: Pope Benedict XVI in the UK* (Darton, Longman & Todd, 2010).

Yet we, like the servants at the wedding feast, must make a change of direction to move from a place of fear or self-interest to a place of joyous celebration and community.

The president of the feast declares, 'Everyone serves good wine first and the worse wine when the guests are well wined; but you have kept the best wine till now.'[33] Jesus is our new wine. This new, yearned for celebration cannot be based on our old choices, but on Christ, our new, life-affirming choice. This is the wine we must offer the world. This is the new wine that God spoke of to the prophet Jeremiah:

> They will come, shouting for joy on the heights of Zion,
> thronging towards Yahweh's lavish gifts,
> for wheat, new wine and oil,
> sheep and cattle;
> they will be like a well-watered garden,
> they will sorrow no more.
> The young girl will then take pleasure in the dance,
> and young men and old alike;
> I shall change their mourning into gladness,
> comfort them, give them joy after their troubles.[34]

Before the wedding feast at Cana, two of John the Baptist's disciples see Jesus and follow him. When he sees them, Jesus asks, 'What do you want?' They answer, 'Rabbi ... where do you live?' Jesus' reply is simple: 'Come and see.'[35] When others seeking answers today ask of Jesus, 'where do you live?', will they find in our parishes jars full of the transformed water of new life? Will they find communities alive with love and celebration, where all are

---

[33] John 2:10.
[34] Jeremiah 31:12–13.
[35] John 1:35–39.

welcome irrespective of class, status, gender or race? Or will they find in our communities empty jars facing inwards, bereft of joy and lacking in hope, where Sunday celebrations have become nothing more than empty and habitual ritual?

This is the question that, as Church gathered together each Sunday, should be uppermost in our mind and at the heart of our parish communities. What sort of Church do we want to be? What sort of Church is Jesus calling us to be? This is the question that Jesus, through all of the seven signs, challenges us to ask of ourselves and each other.

While we must avoid the temptation to spend our time in inward contemplation, for the task that Jesus sets us today is far too important and far too urgent, this is still the question that Jesus asked those first disciples. It is the question that Jesus asked of his mother at the wedding feast at Cana, and now he asks each of us today, 'What do you want from me? What do you want from me?'

2

'Unless you see signs and portents you will not believe!'

The healing of the royal official's son (John 4:46–54)

In the story of the wedding feast at Cana we have seen how Jesus sets us a challenge – 'What do you want from me?' – and that this challenge is firmly placed in the context and calling of the celebration of community. We witness the response of Mary, a response of faith that began with her 'yes' to the messenger of the Lord before the very birth of Jesus. Mary's inspiring faith led the servants of the bridal feast at Cana to action and, in that action, the servants discovered a new and emboldening trust in God which took them out of their place of fear. In the second of the seven signs, the healing of the royal official's son, the beloved disciple leads us on the next part of our journey. Here we are called to explore the nature of faith itself by coming to accept that, even in the intimacy of the relationship to which Jesus calls each of us, we cannot possess the gift of faith without fully embracing the gift of doubt.

The royal official

First, let us remind ourselves of the backdrop before which the second sign occurs. Jesus has returned to Cana, the place of the first sign of his public ministry. Here, on the road, he encounters a royal official from Capernaum. The official tells him that his son is ill and asks Jesus to cure him. He pleads, 'Come down before my child dies.'[1] Jesus tells him to go home and that his son is cured. And so the royal official begins the journey back to Capernaum without question. On returning to his home he finds that his son has indeed recovered and that this healing took place on the seventh hour, the very same time at which Jesus told him that his son was healed. In order to understand how this sign speaks to us today, let us first try to imagine the events that brought the royal official to that moment on the dusty road at Cana and his encounter with Jesus.

What does the beloved disciple tell us about the royal official? We know that he comes from Capernaum and, while we do not know his exact role or position, his title would suggest that he is likely to be a man of status and standing. As such, it is highly probable that he is looked up to by the community in Capernaum, and perhaps even further afield. We can assume that he has a wife and a family and is wealthy enough to command a household with many servants.[2] He has a job and a position at court many would be envious of. He has an income which allows him and his family to want for nothing. He might be described as a pillar of the community, respected and well

---

[1] John 4:49.
[2] John 4:51.

liked. To others, perhaps, he is an object of envy – he has everything. In the context of the time, he may even have near celebrity status.

Then, suddenly and without warning, his world begins to collapse around him. His dearly beloved son, whom he has cherished since birth and in whom he has placed all his hopes and dreams for the future, falls ill. At first he and his wife try not to be too concerned. They hide their worries behind a veneer of false hope and confidence, convincing themselves that this must be nothing more than a minor illness. They cannot admit to themselves the true gravity of the situation. And so they take comfort from every assuring word their doctor may offer. They grasp every single straw of hope that is offered to them, every small sign of improvement, no matter how fleeting it may be. Surely their son will get better soon? Look, they can see a small improvement in his condition – all must be well? But their son's condition does not improve. Slowly, before their eyes, he deteriorates, he is wasting away. Every passing day robs him of another breath of life; every passing day they see his pain increasing; and every passing day they feel the pain of their hearts silently breaking as the fever devours him while they stand by helpless.

They have paid for the finest medical advice their money can buy. Yet now the physicians tell them that their son's condition is untreatable. He will die. It is now only a matter of time; there is nothing they can do; he is beyond all hope.

The news is like a knife piercing their hearts. Their grief is unbearable. Perhaps they blame themselves, or, in their darkest moments, each other. Or perhaps they cling to each other in pain as they watch their son, slowly and inevitably, dying. The official feels forsaken and lost.

He is in utter despair. Despite his wealth, despite his status, he is powerless; there is nothing he can do. He is helpless. His God has deserted his wife and his son. His God has deserted him. In anguish he screams in the quiet of his heart, 'My God, my God, why have you forsaken me?'[3]

For the royal official, there is an added dimension to his grief. José Martí, the hero of Cuban independence, is reported to have said that before he dies every man should plant a tree, write a book and have a son. All of these point to a man leaving something of himself in this world, leaving a heritage which speaks of his existence beyond death. Perhaps, for the royal official, the death of his son marks not only the death of his beloved child but the end of his family line. If that is so, then the thought of his son's death also speaks to his own fragile mortality.

Then, one morning, the royal official awakes and says he is going to travel to Cana in search of a man called Jesus. We do not know what he knows of Jesus; perhaps he has heard the news of the sign at the wedding feast. Perhaps he has heard or witnessed miracles of Jesus himself in Capernaum.[4] His wife is distraught. Is he out of his mind? How can he leave now, when his son is dying? How can he abandon her in the face of death? He is nothing more than an emotional coward who cannot face the death of his son. These accusatory words burn deep into him, stinging like a blade thrust into his side.

But within him, within the deepest reaches of his soul, he knows he must do something. He simply cannot stand

---

[3] Mark 15:34.

[4] John does not place any of the other six signs in Capernaum. However, Luke describes a number of miracles occurring there. See Luke 4:31–41 for the cure of the demoniac, the cure of Simon's mother-in-law and the cure of many suffering from diseases.

by and do nothing. There is an unknown feeling, a hitherto unknown voice deep within him, urging him on to a course of action to which there can be no certain outcome. So he leaves, and as he does so he kisses his son goodbye. He holds on to him, not wanting to let go, fighting back the tears of grief as he realises that he will likely never see him again. He tries to explain to his wife, but she does not want to hear, she cannot hear, she is hysterical with grief.

And so he sets off. The journey is hard. It will take at least two days to reach Cana in the searing heat.[5] There is no guarantee that he will even be able to find this man called Jesus. He is alone with his thoughts on that road to Cana, with only his servants for company. They say nothing, they cannot even look him in the eye lest they betray how they are feeling. Surely the master has gone mad with sorrow that he would now lead them on this fool's errand?

It is in the midst of this anguish, in the midst of this unbearable pain, that he begins to doubt. Is he insane? What has he done? He should return immediately to his home and family. At least he will be able to hold on to and cling to his son as he passes away. Who is this Jesus? What can he do? It is only now, in his foolishness, that he realises that he knows nothing of him. He turned water into wine at Cana – a cheap magician's trick. Why did he ever think that this Nazarene could cure his son? What in heaven's name was he thinking of? He travels towards Cana through the long night, struggling with the unbearable weight of his doubt.

Yet the life of his son is at stake. He is racked with guilt

---

[5] We know the length of the journey because of the timeline of the royal official's journey home, when he realises that his son was cured at least the day before his arrival home.

for leaving his family, but still something is pushing him on his journey, beyond his doubt, some madness he cannot explain. Finally, as the sun rises, he sees Cana in the distance. He is filled with hope, with expectation, but most of all still with doubt. Quickly, he must rush; he must find Jesus.

It is at this point that we enter into the narrative that the beloved disciple tells. The royal official's world has collapsed around him. He is in pain and his heart is breaking with grief. He is full of doubt. And it is on this road of pain, grief and doubt that he finally encounters Jesus.

It is in doubt that we meet Jesus

It is here, too, that Jesus meets us today, on our own personal road to Cana. For many of us, like the royal official, this will be a road of pain, grief and doubt. It is here also that Jesus meets humanity. In a world craving certainty, we are led to believe that doubt is somehow harmful, something to be avoided, something that leads us away from faith. It is this doubt that John Paul II spoke of in his homily on the inauguration of his pontificate: 'So often today, man does not know that which is within him, in the depths of his mind and heart. So often he is uncertain about the meaning of his life on this earth. He is assailed by doubt, a doubt which turns into despair.'[6]

Society teaches us that doubt is wrong. From an early age we are filled with scientific truth in the pursuit of absolute knowledge. Our education is based on a system which teaches us facts and more facts. It does not teach us

---

[6] Pope John Paul II, homily on the occasion of his inauguration to the pontificate.

that unknowing, uncertainty and doubt are values to be cherished.

Yet doubt is part of our human condition. It is how God has created us, as children of faith and children of doubt. In fact, without doubt, without uncertainty, there would be no scientific enquiry, no scientific progress. We would all still believe that the universe rotated around the earth, and that the earth was flat. Without doubt, without uncertainty, there would be no gift of faith. 'Jesus said to him: You believe because you can see me. Blessed are those who have not seen and yet believe.'[7]

Although we are born with this seed of doubt, it is something that makes us feel uncomfortable. To live in doubt is to live in a place in which we do not want to dwell. So we constantly seek certainty in our world and in our environment. Much of our lives could be characterised as a struggle between certainty and doubt, between knowledge and ignorance, and between fact and ambiguity. This struggle finds the centre of the storm in our obsession with choice.

We are certain that we know what is best for our children, the right way to bring them up. Yet every parent struggles with the doubt of whether they are in fact good parents: 'Surely I can do better, I feel so inadequate.' We are certain about the clothes or make-up we want to wear, yet we doubt our own beauty or physical attributes: 'Surely no one is going to find me attractive?' We are certain about the consumer choices we make, and yet we try to bury deep the doubts about the provenance of the goods we buy and whether or not our choices are founded on the economic suffering of others as a result of an unfair global

---

[7] John 20:29.

economic system. We may be certain about the career choices we have made, yet we wonder what is next, we worry about our job security and our ability to pay the bills.

We may be certain about our faith, yet in candid moments we also worry about death, we worry about whether there is a God or just a desolate void of nothingness. And in these worries we may feel empty and alone and even abandoned by God. We may reach out for his loving and tender assurance, but sometimes find nothing but emptiness.

However, like the royal official, it is only in doubt that we will truly encounter Christ. So, as the royal official made his journey from Capernaum to Cana in search of Jesus, so, on our own spiritual journey, we too will encounter doubt and uncertainty. Yet we should not look upon doubt as an enemy of faith, but rather as a precious gift, a loving friend to be embraced.

As we are limited by our human nature and understanding, so our comprehension of God must in itself be limited. We cannot claim to know with any certainty the nature or the essence of our God. If we make a claim to such knowledge, we seek to contain God within the limits of our own intellect and, in so doing, seek to claim parity with him. The secular world argues that through the absolute pursuit of science we can find absolute truth, we can find 'the theory of everything'.[8] If we believe that in our human existence there will always be a provable answer to everything, then we are in danger of becoming like Adam and Eve, giving in to the temptation of eating

---

[8] It was Albert Einstein who searched for a 'unified field theory' that would adequately address both gravity and electromagnetism.

from the tree of knowledge. And in so doing we will, like Adam and Eve, ultimately only find alienation from God as we too are excluded from Eden through our own actions.[9] This is not an argument for a type of pseudo-Christian relativism. There will always be absolute truth. However, our understanding and comprehension of that truth can never be complete.

Walking with doubt

Just as we cannot fully know the nature of God, neither can we fully comprehend the Trinitarian mystery of love which is God. The only thing we can be certain of is doubt! Where there is unknowing, there will always be doubt. To doubt is to be a person of faith; to doubt is to be fully human. It is because of his very humanity that Jesus prayed at the Garden of Gethsemane that the cup of his death might pass him by.[10] And it was because of his very humanity that Jesus cried out at the moment of his death, 'My God, my God, why have you forsaken me?'[11]

It is not by our doubt that we will be measured, but rather by how we respond to that doubt on our journey. Do we give up on our road and head back to our home, to the safety of familiarity? Or do we, like the royal official and with courage in our hearts, press ahead to Cana in search of the Lord?

John tells us that when the royal official encounters Jesus, he immediately asks him to come with him to Capernaum and cure his son. He implores Jesus, 'Come

---

[9] Genesis 3.
[10] Luke 22:42.
[11] Mark 15:34.

down before my child dies.'[12] Jesus instructs him to go home: 'your son will live.'[13] John tells us that on hearing this, the royal official believes what Jesus says and goes on his way. But, as he starts his journey home, let us examine this encounter further.

The royal official has been travelling through the night. His son's life is at stake. He has travelled in despair and pain, yet with the faintest glimmer of hope and expectation to enlighten his night. He knows he must find Jesus; yet when he does, his encounter with Jesus does not last more than a few minutes. Jesus at first rebukes him, saying, 'Unless you see signs and portents you will not believe!'[14] He then sends him on his way with the promise that his son will be cured. At that instant the royal official believes, and begins the journey home. There is something so special in his short encounter with Jesus that, at least in that moment, it wipes away any doubts and uncertainties that he may have had. In that moment he finds faith and certainty in the fact that his son will live. His journey has not been in vain.

Thus, having met Christ, and having believed in his word, the royal official starts his journey home. He is, however, only human. How long would it have been, as he walked that now familiar road home, before the doubts and uncertainties resurfaced? A nagging doubt: perhaps he would arrive home to find his son's condition had deteriorated or, even worse, to find his son dead? We cannot blame the royal official for this. Even Peter, who had known Jesus intimately throughout his public ministry,

[12] John 4:49.
[13] John 4:50.
[14] John 4:48.

was so fuelled by fear and doubt that he denied him three times.[15] It is, therefore, not unreasonable for us to find the royal official with doubts, misgivings and fears. He has encountered the Lord and he is full of a newly found exuberant faith. Now, however, on the lonely road home, nagging, whispering voices of uncertainty begin to re-emerge.

Perhaps it is only when he encounters his servants coming out to meet him with the news that his son is cured that he begins to feel the certainty of faith again. But, even upon hearing this joyful news, he still does not truly believe. His son has been cured, yes, but is this really the work of Jesus? He is prompted to ask at what time his son was cured. His servants respond that his fever left him the previous day at the seventh hour. It is only then that the royal official, realising that this is the exact time when Jesus said his son would live, truly believes. His initial faith in Jesus is reconfirmed.

How terrible it is to be without God

The story of the royal official's journey of faith speaks to us. If we consider our first real adult encounter with Christ, we are filled with the wonder, awe and joy of new-found faith. It is like the first flush of love, the beginning of a new relationship where everything seems possible and we are filled with excitement, passion and hope. In the wonder of such love we are consumed with a certainty of hope and action. Our lives seem forever changed. Yet, over time, since that moment, perhaps we have suffered qualms

---

[15] John 18:15–27.

and uncertainties. We are filled sometimes with the worries of our lives and in times of doubt and anguish we may feel lost and abandoned. We look for signs from the Lord to confirm our flagging faith. Like the royal official, we have met the Lord, but this does not mean we can banish doubt in our lives.

This sense of doubt, of being forsaken by God, has been central to the faith experience of many of the great saints of the Church. St John of the Cross first wrote of what he described as the 'dark night of the soul' as being a necessary part of the faith journey of all Christians who have encountered Jesus. He likened its purpose to that of a mother rearing her child. At first, a loving mother will breastfeed her child and caress it in her arms. However, as the child grows older she weans it from her breast and sets it down from her arms, allowing the child to walk on its own.[16] So it is with our relationship with God. At first we are cradled in the experiential tenderness and intimacy of God's love. Yet, as we grow in our faith, we must let go and begin to walk the harder path of our faith journey. St Paul recognised this when he wrote, 'When I was a child, I used to talk like a child, and see things as a child does, and think like a child; but now that I have become an adult, I have finished with all childish ways.'[17]

St John of the Cross wrote in *The Dark Night of the Soul* that it is only by going through the 'passive night of the senses' and the 'passive night of the spirit', where the pilgrim is robbed of the experiential and spiritual sense of God, that we are created anew on our spiritual journey

---

[16] *The Collected Works of St John of the Cross*, translated by Kieran Kavanaugh OCD and Otilio Rodriguez OCD (ISP Publications, 1991), *The Dark Night of the Soul*, Book One, chapter 1.
[17] 1 Corinthians 13:11.

with God. When the seeker empties himself, to the extent that he lets go of his own experience of a personal God, then a person can begin to truly know God. Often this doubt has been experienced so intensely as to be an almost physical pain or yearning. Of such a traveller through the dark night John wrote:

> They resemble one who is imprisoned in a dark dungeon, bound hands and feet, and able neither to move nor see nor feel any favour from heaven or earth. They remain in this condition until their spirit is humbled, softened and purified, until it becomes so delicate, simple and refined that it can be at one with the Spirit of God.[18]

St John of the Cross went further and likened the dark night of the soul to a painful experience involving 'many fears, imaginings and struggles'.[19]

This spiritual struggle has been experienced by many of the greatest saints of the Church. But in this struggle they have found a deeper loving relationship with God. In the midst of illness the young St Thérèse of Lisieux experienced something of the 'dark night'. She wrote that following one Easter celebration in which she had had an intense, almost physical, experience of Christ calling her to her death – a call that she eagerly wished to respond to in joy – God had then 'allowed' her soul to be overwhelmed with darkness.[20] She likened this to having been born in a land of thick fogs where she had never seen the beauties of nature or a single ray of sunlight. Although she had believed from childhood that, even in the darkness,

---

[18] *The Dark Night of the Soul*, Book Two, chapter 8.
[19] Ibid., Book Two, chapter 9.
[20] *Story of a Soul: The Three-Person'd God – The Autobiography of St Thérèse of Lisieux*, chapter ix (1996).

another and more beautiful country was awaiting her, overwhelmed by the spiritual darkness she wrote:

> When my heart, weary of the surrounding darkness, tries to find some rest in the thought of a life to come, my anguish increases. It seems to me that out of the darkness I hear the mocking voice of the unbeliever: 'You dream of a land of light and fragrance, you dream that the Creator of these wonders will be yours for ever, you think one day to escape from these mists where you now languish. Nay, rejoice in death, which will give you, not what you hope for, but a night darker still, the night of utter nothingness!'[21]

Nevertheless, notwithstanding the painful doubts that assailed her, and perhaps even because of them, St Thérèse wrote that never before had she felt so deeply how sweet and merciful the Lord is.

St Thérèse of Lisieux was not alone in her spiritual pain. Mother Teresa, the foundress of the Missionaries of Charity, was to many people a light in the darkness of our world. From the moment she entered the slums of Calcutta in December 1948, to her death on 5 September 1997, she was a witness, a beacon of Christ's love and compassion for the poor, the displaced and the sick – not only for those in the city of Calcutta in India, but for all those living in grinding poverty. Her example helped millions of people grow in the faith and love of Christ, and has inspired thousands of men and women to follow her in religious life.

Yet, on the publication of many of her private letters in 2007, the world was amazed to find out that, except for a short reprieve in 1959, almost from the beginning of her

---

[21] Ibid.

life tending the poor until her death in 1997 she, too, suffered the long dark night of the soul. Published in *Mother Teresa Come Be My Light*,[22] many of her letters, written to her spiritual directors, reveal a woman who was racked with doubt and who spoke of being in darkness and alone from God. This was not simply some dry or barren patch of prayer, but a deep inner emptiness devoid of any feeling of God.

> I have nothing – since I have not got Him – whom my heart & soul longs to possess ... – nothing enters my soul ... If there is hell – this must be one. How terrible it is to be without God – no prayer – no faith – no love.[23]

Like St Thérèse of Lisieux, in the midst of this pain and anguish Mother Teresa, through her 'unfeeling' faith, wished to lay her life at the disposal of God, to do his service, to be attendant at his feet, to give herself totally to Christ.

> And yet, Father – in spite of all these – I want to be faithful to Him – to spend myself for Him, to love Him, not for what He gives but for what He takes – to be at his disposal – I do not ask Him to change His attitude towards me or His plans for me. – I only ask Him to use me.[24]

Both Thérèse and Teresa in their doubt and emptiness, although they were devoid of a physical feeling of God, reaffirmed their faith in their lives, believing not just with their hearts but with their minds. It was in this doubt-led faith that they encountered a deeper understanding and knowledge of the love of God. It was in this doubt-led faith

---

[22] *Mother Teresa Come Be My Light*, edited and commentary by Brian Kolodiejchuk MC (Rider, 2007).
[23] Ibid.
[24] Ibid.

that they emptied themselves to the service of God – to be truly and wholeheartedly at his disposal. It is here, perhaps, that we can begin to understand fully the true meaning, power and challenge of the words of our risen Jesus to the apostles: 'You believe because you can see me. Blessed are those who have not seen and yet believe.'[25]

Thankfully, the vast majority of us will not be called upon to endure the long dark night of the soul that St Thérèse of Lisieux and Mother Teresa suffered. Yet we will all suffer moments of darkness, our own small dark nights, periods of aloneness, of despair, of emptiness. Like the royal official on his lonely road to Cana, we will all experience moments of uncertainty when we stare into the void. It is part of our human condition; it is part of our own journey of faith. And it is in those moments that God calls us, like Thérèse and Teresa, to be truly and wholeheartedly at his disposal.

Unless you see signs and portents you will not believe!

Before we leave the story of the second sign, let us turn back to the words of Jesus to the royal official. Again, as in Cana where Jesus addresses his mother Mary, when the royal official asks him to come to Capernaum to heal his son, Jesus seems to rebuke him. Jesus' words seem to be far from compassionate to a man whose son is dying. He says, 'Unless you see signs and portents you will not believe!'[26] However, let us put Jesus' words into context.

[25] John 20:29.
[26] John 4:48.

As we have seen, his public ministry began at the wedding feast at Cana. In the beloved disciple's narrative, since that event Jesus has already travelled to and preached in Jerusalem. There, he threw out the traders and merchants from the temple – showing the Jewish people the radical nature of the new Kingdom to which God was calling them. He has spoken at length with Nicodemus, one of the respected Pharisees, and in that discourse revealed himself as the light of the world. He has also ministered in Judea. However, immediately before arriving back in Cana (in Galilee) he has spent time in Samaria. Only amongst the Samaritans, who were regarded by the Jewish people with distrust as outsiders, does Jesus find those who believe in him not on the strength of miracles, but because of his words and, indeed for some, because of the testimony of others.

So it is in Cana, back amongst his own Jewish people, that Jesus speaks to the royal official in such seemingly harsh terms. In this context perhaps we might mistake words of sadness and disappointment for words of rebuke. They are words of sadness and disappointment because, unlike the Samaritans, his own people do not understand the reality of who he really is. They do not understand the reality of the new Kingdom to which God is calling them. And they do not comprehend that, while it is true that the new Kingdom Jesus is heralding is accompanied by miraculous signs and portents, these signs and portents are not in themselves the central message of Jesus' ministry and the new Kingdom. The central message is, rather, about new life to be found in belief in Jesus and a new Kingdom, a Kingdom established both in heaven and on earth, based on love, peace and justice. Here is Jesus saying what we might paraphrase in today's idiom as, 'You know what? You guys just don't get it!'

What is Jesus saying to us, the Church, today? When we look for modern-day 'signs and portents', we are perhaps looking for spiritual and religious certainty. Some of us may look for the performance of miracles to convince us of what we struggle to believe. It is not surprising that so many are attracted to the growing fundamentalist and evangelical churches throughout the world. Some of us may find shelter and comfort in the certainty of all Church teaching. We have allowed our society, which preaches instant gratification, to impinge upon our faith experience. We seek instant signs of faith, or instant security within dogma and doctrine.

Our faith is founded on certain and absolute fundamental truths: for example, who Jesus is, the nature of the sacramental gifts we receive and the basis of apostolic authority. However, there is a danger that, in trying to shoehorn all facets of our faith and tradition into a box entitled 'Fundamental and Certain Truth', we lose all sense of the reality of who God is and his plan for each one of us and the Church.

In so doing we adopt a fundamentalist approach to belief in which there is no room for doubt and no room for others' views or perspectives. If we take this approach, we risk becoming entrenched in positions and certainties, which leads us to elevate all aspects of our belief to the position of fundamental and necessary dogma in which there is no room for God himself. Nor do we leave room for the revealing and creating work of the Holy Spirit, either in our lives or the life of the Church.

In his book *God In All Things*, Gerard Hughes argues that 'Complete religious certainty about God without any shadow of doubt is a sign of atheism. The God we think we know all about cannot be the true God, because God is always greater than our powers of comprehension.'[27]

Absolute religious certainty, without room for doubt, leads inevitably to religious fundamentalism with its absolute claim on truth. Such a path can lead us only away from God rather than closer to him. It is the path that led to the Spanish Conquistadors' destruction of the Aztec empire. It is the path that led to the murder of thousands of Catholics and Protestants in Northern Ireland and it is the path that led to the thousands of lives being lost on 11 September 2001 with the destruction of the World Trade Center.

Jesus demands of us another way. True belief and faith demands of itself true uncertainty and doubt. Yes, we are called to be a faithful Church, but we are also called to be a Church that does not offer fundamentalist positions on all matters of faith. We are called to be a Church that offers faith but embraces doubt, for it is only in both faith and doubt that the world can encounter Jesus. So what, then, are the characteristics of a doubt-led Church?

First, we must acknowledge that we, as the Church, do not have a complete monopoly on truth. This requires a humbleness of spirit, a recognition that while we hold on to certain fundamental truths, we are sinning against God if we believe that we are the sole custodians of all truth or that we can contain the totality of God within the bounds of what we call doctrine or dogma. It was in this humbleness of spirit that the Church recognised in the Second Vatican Council that many elements of sanctification and truth are found outside the visible structure of the

---

[27] Gerard W. Hughes, *God In All Things* (Hodder and Stoughton, 2003).

Church.[28] Doctrine leads us to God but can never contain the totality of the personhood of God. We live our lives in a 'mystery of faith'.

Second, we must acknowledge that we cannot offer the secular world complete certainty of faith. As attractive as it might be in the face of aggressive atheism, we cannot deliver Jesus up as a ready-made package. What we can, and must, do is to accompany humanity on a journey of faith where, in the search, we will encounter the risen Christ. On this journey we can and must witness to the truth of our beliefs, not only through the central teachings of the Church but, primarily, through our actions based on such teachings. At the core of that witness of action there must be a service of love. On that journey, too, we must recognise that we will meet women and men of different views and beliefs from us – women and men who, nonetheless, can teach us something of the love and reality of God.

Finally, we must as a Church have an open and listening heart. This open and listening heart must be at the centre of our communities, our parishes, our deaneries and dioceses. It is the heart which holds at its core what Archbishop Vincent Nichols described in his homily, on the occasion of his installation as the new Archbishop of Westminster, as a 'respectful dialogue'. This respectful dialogue must engage all: within our communities and without, with the churched and the unchurched, with believers of all faiths and believers of none.

> Respectful dialogue is crucial today and I salute all who seek to engage in it ... Let us be a society in which we genuinely listen to each other, in which sincere

---

[28] *Lumen Gentium*, chapter 1, 'The Mystery of the Church', 8.

disagreement is not made out to be insult or harassment, in which reasoned principles are not construed as prejudice and in which we are prepared to attribute to each other the best and not the worst of motives. In these matters, we ourselves in the churches have so much to learn and do.[29]

In entering into a respectful dialogue with the world, with an open heart and with an ear of faith, we may soon become aware of our own individual and collective shortcomings and failings as the body of Christ gathered together as Church. This may cause us to doubt not only our faith, but our worthiness to be called followers of Christ. Yet it is how we respond to such doubts that will determine how faithful and faith-led we are as a community. Where we do not doubt, we deny our own humanity and in so doing we deny the humanity of the Church. With closed hearts of certainty and truth we become like the Pharisees. We leave no room for the ever-creative and imaginative workings of the Holy Spirit.

In the 2005 Pulitzer Prize-winning play *Doubt: A Parable* by John Patrick Shanley,[30] the two central characters, Sister Aloysius and Father Flynn, are in a battle over the truth. Sister Aloysius is in a state of sure and certain belief. In her mind she knows that Father Flynn is abusing one of the boys in his charge. Of this there can be no doubt. She is utterly convinced. Yet, as the audience, we are not so sure of the truth of these allegations and, within the play, their veracity or otherwise is never confirmed. Father Flynn vehemently denies them and there is little more than circumstantial evidence surrounding them. Nevertheless,

---

[29] Homily of Archbishop Vincent Nichols, given on the date of his installation at Westminster Cathedral, 21 May 2009.
[30] John Patrick Shanley, *Doubt: A Parable* (Theatre Communications Group, Inc., 2005).

Sister Aloysius is convinced of the truth of the allegations and of her own certainty and she vigorously pursues Father Flynn, determined to have him removed from the parish.

In their final confrontation, Father Flynn says to her in desperation, 'Sister, remember that there are circumstances beyond your knowledge. Even if you feel certainty, it is an emotion and not a fact.'[31] Sister Aloysius, in her relentless pursuit to prove the truth of her allegations, admits that she will stop at nothing to prove Father Flynn's guilt, even if it means that she must step outside the Church and be 'dammed to hell'.[32] In the end she resorts to lying, fabricating a conversation with a nun in Father Flynn's previous parish. Finally Father Flynn feels he has no option but to leave.

Even though we do not know the truth or otherwise of the events that have occurred, we are left with little sympathy for Sister Aloysius but much empathy for Father Flynn. In him we see a man of love and compassion. However, regarding Sister Aloysius and her dogged pursuit of truth, no matter what the cost and no matter by what means, we are left with the picture of a woman who has no charity or compassion, a cold, vindictive woman who is trapped by her own sense of self-righteousness.

It is only in the closing words of the final scene of the play that we find any empathy with her and begin to see her humanity and weakness. For her final words find resonance in the quiet of our hearts. As she breaks down and confesses to Sister James, her young novice, that she has lied, bent with emotion she declares, 'I have doubts! I have such doubts!'[33]

---

[31] Ibid.
[32] Ibid.
[33] Ibid.

Like the royal official, let us, with courage in the midst of our doubt, rise up to meet the Lord on the road to Cana. May he keep us faithful to his path.

3

'I have no one to put me into the pool when the water is disturbed'

The healing on the Sabbath at Bethesda (John 5:1-18)

We have seen in the first two signs the importance of the celebration of community and faith. We have also witnessed the recognition that with faith we will encounter doubt. Yet by embracing doubt we are being true to ourselves and to humanity, and to the call of Christ. It is in our living of this truth every day that we encounter Jesus on our own road to Cana. So what does the third of Jesus' signs reveal to us? There are two parts to the story of the healing of the sick man on the Sabbath at Bethesda: first, the cure of the sick man, and second, the reaction of the Jewish authorities to that healing. Let us continue our journey by looking at how the story begins.

The Kingdom is at hand

We are told that, following the healing of the royal official's son, Jesus travelled on to Jerusalem. Here, at the pool at Bethesda,[1] many blind, lame and crippled people gathered daily, waiting to be cured by immersing themselves in the waters. It is in this crowd of those in need that Jesus sees a man who has been paralysed for thirty-eight years.[2] John explains that Jesus realises the man has been in that condition for a long time.[3] When Jesus approaches the man, he asks whether he wants to be well. The man responds by telling Jesus that he has no one to help him get down to the pool when the water is stirred up. It was the held belief that at the moment of stirring the water possessed healing powers. In response Jesus tells him, 'Get up, pick up your sleeping-mat and walk around.'[4] On hearing these words the man is immediately cured and does as Jesus tells him.

So how does the sign speak to us today? On one level we can see Jesus healing the sick, the second time in the Gospel of John where this occurs, a further sign of God's love for us, a further sign of the Kingdom of God made present to the people of Israel. However, as we can see, there inevitably lies beneath John's story a deeper narrative which speaks to us beyond the wonder of the miraculous cure. To understand that narrative we should first look at the circumstances in which this sign takes place.

---

[1] Bethesda comes from the Hebrew word meaning 'House of Mercy' – a theme that the story draws us towards.

[2] See Deuteronomy 2:14. The significance of thirty-eight years should not be lost. The people of Israel wandered lost in the desert for thirty-eight years. It was only when the entire generation of those of an age to bear arms was eliminated that the promise concerning the Promised Land could begin to be fulfilled.

[3] John 5:6.

[4] John 5:8.

Unlike the cure of the royal official's son, this healing takes place in person; it is immediate and visible for all to see, including the Jewish authorities. By contrast, few of the witnesses to the encounter of the royal official and Jesus at Cana will have seen the whole dramatic story of that meeting play out. It is only the royal official, and the servants who have travelled with him, who will have seen the immediacy of the healing of the royal official's son when he arrives home at Capernaum. However, the healing at Bethesda is immediate *and* witnessed by all. We will turn to the consequences for Jesus of that witness later, but here the first point to note is that the healing of the sick man at Bethesda is a very visible and public sign for all to see. It is in the 'now' of history, it is a sign of God's immediate intervention, a sign of God's immediate power, and tellingly, it is a sign that takes place at the 'House of Mercy'.

At Bethesda Jesus reveals to us the special nature of his Kingdom. It is a Kingdom that is here, now, in the present. It is not to be looked forward to as some heavenly reward for a life well lived. It is also a Kingdom in stark contrast to that which would have been known to the Jewish people suffering under Roman rule. That kingdom was built on political power and force. The first public sign of the healing power of Jesus' Kingdom,[5] which brings him into confrontation with the Jewish authorities, occurs not amongst kings and princes but amidst the poor, the sick and the dying at Bethesda. And here is the first and truly amazing aspect of the sign. It is not so much the *what* or *how* of the healing, but rather the *who*. It is Jesus who

---

[5] While it may be argued that the sign at the wedding feast at Cana was the first public sign, it occurred at an event to which not all were invited. Furthermore, John gives us no indication that it was within the purview of the Jewish authorities.

focuses our attention on the person of the sick man who is healed and, by so doing, Jesus reveals to us more about the love of the Father, the nature of his Kingdom and his call to us today.

Why the sick man at Bethesda?

Our natural sympathy and concern for the sick in our society may lead us to have an overly romantic view of the sick man at Bethesda. When we see the sick gathered in pilgrimage in places such as Lourdes, our hearts naturally desire to reach out to them. We feel for their pain and suffering. However, this means we risk paying little or no attention to who they are, but rather focus on their condition. In so doing we are in danger of robbing them of their humanity, identifying them by an illness or a disability rather than as the created daughters and sons of the Father and, accordingly, as our own equal sisters and brothers.

But what do we really know about this sick man at Bethesda? The truth is, very little. We do know that he is one of the multitudes of sick and injured lying by the pool at Bethesda. He is surrounded by a mass of the ailing, all of whom have gathered hoping to be cured by immersing themselves in the pool. They are likely to be of all ages, young and old, and all with different illnesses or disabilities. So why does Jesus pick this particular man? Is he a man of special faith or virtue, an example, perhaps, to his fellow sufferers? Or perhaps his illness is so great compared to those around him that his cure will give even greater glory to God?

There is nothing in the story to indicate that either of these is the case, or, indeed, even that this nameless man has any personal experience of or belief in God. One could say that the opposite is more likely to be true. What faith and hope he does have appears to be centred not upon God, but upon the expectation of a cure for himself. It is a self-centred conviction and expectation in which his needs take precedence above all others. It is certainly not a faith that reaches out to others. We are given no indication that this man spends his time in prayer for others, or trying to help, even in some small way, those who are ill around him. The yearning for his cure has become his god and, like the worship of all false idols, it leads him away from the one true God. Thus, as we shall see, it is perhaps unsurprising that he gives a less than gracious response to Jesus' question of whether he wants to be healed, a response which is focused purely on himself.

Does he then have a special faith in Jesus? Does he reach out to Jesus in hope and expectation? Again the narrative gives us no indication of this. Unlike the royal official, who set off on his tortured journey of faith in search of Jesus, actively seeking him out, here the man is passive. He sits waiting, perhaps even too preoccupied with his own thoughts to notice Jesus. It is Jesus who, on seeing him, seeks him out. It is Jesus who actively, and with purpose, reaches out to him.

Moreover, when Jesus speaks to him, he does not preface his healing with a question testing the man's faith. This is in stark contrast to the encounter of Jesus with the royal official at Cana, where Jesus went as far as to rebuke him over his lack of faith: 'Unless you see signs and portents you will not believe.'[6] In contrast, here, Jesus does not ask the man whether he believes in God, let alone

---

[6] John 4:48.

whether he believes in him, Jesus. He simply asks, 'Do you want to be well again?'[7] At Bethesda there is no precondition or requirement of faith. However, what is interesting is the question which Jesus asks. At first sight it may appear insensitive. Here is a man Jesus knows has been sick for thirty-eight years: to ask whether he wants to get better may seem, to say the least, pastorally blunt. Yet perhaps Jesus, in asking the question, is seeking to draw out the nature and personality of the sick man for all to see. Before his healing takes place, Jesus seeks to open up the man.

And so the man's response to the simple question which Jesus asks begins to reveal his state of mind and character. He does not reply with a petitioning 'yes'. It is more of a complaint. 'I have been here for all this time,' he says, 'but because of my condition I can't beat others in getting down to the water quickly enough!' We will later discover that the man's response to his cure is consistent with his first response. It is not one of gratitude, nor is it one which leads him to protect Jesus from the Jewish authorities when they ask questions about Jesus' actions on the Sabbath. So what is it, then, about this man that Jesus should pick him out from the multitude of the sick at Bethesda? Why is this seemingly undeserving and unlikeable man chosen?

While we know that the man has been paralysed for thirty-eight years, we do not know for how many years he has been coming to the pool at Bethesda, hoping and yearning for a cure. Through those long years he has probably suffered not only physically but emotionally. He will have been discriminated against and outcast from

---

[7] John 5.6

religious society, as for many his disability would have been equated with either his own personal sin or that of his forebears. As we shall see in the sixth sign, it was this philosophy that led the apostles to ask Jesus whether the young man was born blind because of his sins or the sins of his parents. We also know that he sits by the pool alone: 'I have no one to put me into the pool when the water is disturbed.'[8] Perhaps he has no family, or they have abandoned him – either because they cannot afford to support him or, worse still, they are embarrassed by the shame that his illness brings upon them.

Each day that he sits there by the pool at Bethesda, in expectation and hope, he has suffered bitter disappointment as he watches some of those around him being cured. Yet it is never his turn. Without the help of others, he cannot reach the waters as they begin to stir. So he sits surrounded by the rush of the multitude scrambling, pushing past him, perhaps even knocking him down as the crowd struggle to get to the pool first. And, in the midst of this rush, in the midst of this multitude, he is alone and forlorn. He is ignored and has become exiled from those around him. To many, if not all, he has become invisible and faceless. In the narrative he is quite literally nameless. We are reminded of the words of David: 'Look on my right and see – there is no one who recognises me. All refuge is denied me, no one cares whether I live or die.'[9]

The crowd surrounding him do not know who he is, and they are very likely not even aware of his presence. Sitting amidst this huge crowd, he is alone, he has become separated and alienated from his own community, the very

---

[8] John 5:7.
[9] Psalm 142:4.

community in which he lives. He is one of the multitudes of the unnoticed, of the lost, of the estranged. In this mass of the unnamed, perhaps he has even begun to lose his own sense of identity, his own sense of worth. His condition has become his identity, his defining characteristic. He has become lost from his true self. It is, therefore, unsurprising that his first response to Jesus is as it is. It is a response focused on his need above, and even to the detriment of, all others.

Perhaps this is the very reason why Jesus seeks out this unnamed, faceless man at Bethesda without any precondition of faith. It is not because he is physically ill – there is a multitude of the sick at Bethesda, many, according to the world's values, much more deserving than him. It is not because he has faith in God or even in Jesus himself. It is not because he is a man of virtue and honour. No, it is because he is alone and alienated from those around him. He is one solitary face amongst a sea of faces. Yet in and through his encounter with Jesus, his forgotten story comes to life. His life takes on new meaning, new identity – and, through the sign of his cure, Jesus shows us the love and compassion of our God and demonstrates that the new Kingdom is open to all.

Living on the island

In the movie based on the Nick Hornby book of the same name, *About a Boy*, we encounter the central protagonist, Will. He has lived much of his life up till now avoiding real intimacy with others. He prefers to live a solitary self-indulgent existence where he is free to do what he wants, when he wants. Parodying the metaphysical poet John

Donne, he views himself as a completely self-sufficient individual, reliant only upon the trappings of modern living which are under his control:

> In my opinion, all men are islands. And what's more, now's the time to be one. This is an island age. A hundred years ago, you had to depend on other people. No one had TV or CDs or DVDs or videos ... or home espresso makers. Actually, they didn't have anything cool. Whereas now, you see ... you can make yourself a little island paradise.[10]

Most of us will experience 'island living' at some time in our lives. On occasions we may even crave and seek out the solitude of the island. However, for some of us, perhaps our experience of living on the island is not such a happy one. In the clamour and crowds of our own lives, sometimes we may feel like the man at Bethesda, lost and alone, alienated from our families, our community and our God.

During the rush hour, on my commute to work in the City, I witness daily a multitude of people rushing to get to their place of work on time. Faces are down, no one dares make eye contact. All our thoughts are turned inwards: focusing on the needs of the day; focusing on real worries and problems; focusing, perhaps, on difficult or broken relationships, on a bill that cannot be paid, on an illness more serious than originally thought, or the impending loss of a job and its attendant security.

These concerns, all real and valid, can become, for a moment, our individual defining points of identity. Rarely a smile is seen; rarely a person reaches out to another with a simple 'hello' or 'good morning'. That is not the etiquette

---

[10] The movie *About a Boy* was produced in 2002, based on Nick Hornby's book *About a Boy* (Victor Gollancz Ltd, 1998).

of the rush hour. Although surrounded by thousands of people, all of whom work in the same community as I do, many of whom live in the same community as my family and I, the journey to work is a lonely and alienating experience. Turned in on ourselves, on our own worries and concerns, for a moment we are alienated not only from ourselves but from each other and God. We forget, in that moment, that we are part of a greater whole. We forget, in that moment, a fundamental truth about our human existence. It was this truth, parodied by Will, that led the poet John Donne to write:

> No man is an island, entire of itself;
> every man is a piece of the continent, a part of the main.
> If a clod be washed away by the sea,
> Europe is the less, as well as if a promontory were,
> as well as if a manor of thy friend's or of thine own were:
> any man's death diminishes me, because I am involved in mankind,
> and therefore never send to know for whom the bell tolls;
> it tolls for thee.[11]

We may be lucky enough only to experience this culture of alienation, the culture of 'the island', for short periods in our lives. But for many people, like the man at Bethesda, their whole lives are lived in this moment, on 'the island'. Their experience of the world is one of loneliness, of being one of the millions of the faceless in our society whose lives have been forgotten or have become defined by the crisis of their existence, rather than by the beauty of their own creation and self. These are the alienated and alone of our world. If we open our eyes we will see them in our

---

[11] John Donne, Meditation no. 17, *Devotions Upon Emergent Occasions* (1624).

workplace, in our street, in our parishes, and perhaps even in our own homes.

Every day we may hear or engage in talk about them, but such talk inevitably has the risk of categorising the alone into neat bundles where their existence can be comfortably removed from our own. For instance, we hear of the millions of unemployed; we hear of the tens of thousands of homeless; we hear of the thousands of children in care. They may be fleetingly in our thoughts, but they are not present to us: they are removed from our everyday experience of the world. Our information age leads us to talk in terms of numbers and statistics and yet, in so doing, we forget and remove ourselves from the very real lives of each of the individuals who go to make up the mass of those numbers.

When we hear or speak of the millions of unemployed, we are in danger of removing ourselves from our neighbour: the father struggling to find work so that he can feed and clothe his young family and keep them above the poverty line. When we hear of the tens of thousands of homeless, we are in danger of removing ourselves from the young teenage girl we see sleeping rough on the streets of London, surrounded by drug addicts and vulnerable to sexual predators, but who would rather live that life than return to the abusive home from which she escaped. When we hear of the thousands of children and young people lost in our care systems, we are in danger of removing ourselves from the young boy in our children's school or club, taken into care because his mother is an alcoholic and his father lives a life of petty crime – a young boy who is deemed too old to find adoptive parents and who will now never know the joy of a childhood lived in the safety and love of a nurturing family.

When we label those who are alone as statistics, no matter how well meaning our intentions, we place ourselves in danger of forgetting that behind each number there lies the story of a unique human life, a unique person, a unique gift from God. In so doing we not only help to contribute to their alienation, but we lose something of our true and better selves, both on the personal and the communal level. In that process we forget the better and true part of our identity, the part which is capable of transcending our own self and reaching out in love towards others.

Here, perhaps, is the first of the messages to be learnt from the cure of the man at Bethesda. It is a message which directs us to re-evaluate our own particular view of the world; to go beyond the multitude and look at the individuals within it and, in so doing, to walk with them rather than remove ourselves from them. Through his choice of the man at Bethesda, Jesus calls us to recognise that we are all part of the whole, all part of a common humanity, all connected to one another as his adopted brothers and sisters and as the sons and daughters of the Father.

Many may argue that this is, in essence, no more than a secular political view.[12] But in reaching out to the sick man at Bethesda, Jesus shows us that the requirement for us to reach out beyond ourselves is part of the divine plan of the Kingdom for each of us. This divine plan is integral to our baptismal mission. It is also part of the divine plan of the Kingdom for the Church, integral to her mission on earth. If we cannot reach out to the alone and the lost, then we

---

[12] Marx spoke of the alienation of mankind being a necessary product of a capitalist system and maintained that such alienation could only be overcome through the application of a socialist state.

cannot reach out to God. God has given each of us the essential 'capacity for transcendence':

> Man cannot give himself to a purely human plan for reality, to an abstract ideal or to a false utopia. As a person, he can give himself to another person or to other persons, and ultimately to God, who is the author of his being and who alone can fully accept his gift.[13]

To fail to recognise and exercise this gift leads to alienation from ourselves, our community and, ultimately, from God:

> A man is alienated if he refuses to transcend himself and to live the experience of selfgiving and of the formation of an authentic human community oriented towards his final destiny, which is God.[14]

To turn from ourselves towards others is the challenge we are set by Jesus at Bethesda. But what does this mean for us individually at a practical level? Faced with such an enormous challenge, what must we do? In addition, if we consider who we are called to reach out to, this will inevitably be a difficult and uncomfortable process. Timothy Radcliffe, in his book *Why Go To Church?*, describes those whom we, as Church and society, alienate, those whom we push 'outside the camp':

> Who are the people outside the camp in our society, the unclean lepers, the prostitutes and tax collectors? Hoodies, street gangs, people luring young men and women into prostitution, MPs caught fiddling their expenses? The supreme unclean in our society is perhaps the paedophile

---

[13] *Centesimus Annus*, paragraph 41.
[14] Ibid.

... who is seen as the very epitome of evil, the scapegoat on whom we load all our fear and failure.[15]

How can we love those whom, in our own limited capacity, we would view as unlovable? How can we accept them as Jesus did? We must consider any internal emotional opposition that we might face. The most important lesson we must learn is the requirement to understand our own personal limitations. We must realise that we are imperfect beings who cannot on our own change the world overnight. Again, the story of the sign at Bethesda has much to teach us.

Surely this is stony ground on which to build the Kingdom?

Let us return to the character of the man at Bethesda, but this time from a perspective after his first meeting with Jesus. We know that on both occasions at Cana those who encountered Jesus were changed. Following an encounter with Jesus, they found courage to act upon a new gift of faith even in the face of adversity. Thus the servants in the midst of the feast are emboldened to act upon the words of Mary, to abandon their tasks to follow what might seem to others a foolish endeavour. In so doing they ignore the possibility that their master may be enraged by their actions. Then, on the dusty road from Capernaum, the royal official is given the courage to start his journey home in the hope and expectation that his beloved son will be cured – ignoring the understandable doubts that might persist in both his heart and mind.

---

[15] Timothy Radcliffe, *Why Go To Church?* (Continuum, 2008).

So what of the sick man at Bethesda? We have already seen that this man, by our own judgemental standards, was likely not the most deserving of those gathered at Bethesda. He comes from a place and experience of a life lived in anger and disappointment. Does his encounter with Jesus change him? Certainly, on the physical level there is a very real change. Jesus has healed him; he is able to get up and walk; he is cured. He acts upon the words of Jesus: 'Get up, pick up your sleeping-mat and walk around.'[16]

This very action in itself would have taken a certain kind of courage: a courage to act upon the words of Jesus, a man he does not know, and a courage to hope, to dream that this cure might actually be true – a courage, to paraphrase President Barack Obama, to have 'the audacity of faith'.[17] If the beloved disciple's narrative had ended there, we would have been left with a warm, positive view of that man. However, if we read on, we discover a man who is depicted as being less deserving of our sympathy. What is remarkable about the story is that, following the initial euphoria and joy of being cured, there is no real indication that the man's encounter with Jesus has changed him on any level other than the purely physical.

From the man there is no sign of gratitude or thanks towards Jesus. His life has been changed forever, turned upside down. His hope and dream of thirty-eight years has come true, and yet he does not even stop to thank Jesus. He is silent. Compare this to the attitude of the Samaritan leper who returns to Jesus, falls prostrate at his feet and

[16] John 5:8.
[17] Barack Obama, *The Audacity of Hope* (Canongate Books, 2007).

thanks him for curing him.[18] Surely there must be something redeeming about the behaviour of the man we encounter at Bethesda?

Has the man had a conversion of the heart, found a new belief in God or Jesus? Again, there is no evidence that this is the case. This is in stark contrast to the royal official, who, on hearing the news of his son's healing and realising that he was cured at exactly the hour Jesus said he was, believes. Not only does he believe, but from that moment his entire household comes to believe in Jesus.[19] Yet here at Bethesda, there is no suggestion that Jesus' encounter with the man has led him to a change of heart or to a renewal or deepening of faith.

In the excitement of the moment, the man has done exactly what Jesus has told him to do. However, in so doing, the man has contravened the Sabbath law. The Sabbath was considered holy by the Jewish people. The Sabbath, meaning 'rest', derived its holiness from the creation story in Genesis, where God rested on the seventh day and made it holy.[20] This was echoed not only in the feeding of the Jewish people with manna and quails in the desert, where the Lord commanded that the seventh day be a day of complete rest, a day sacred to the Lord,[21] but also in the commandments given to Moses by the Lord on Mount Sinai: 'Remember the Sabbath day and keep it holy. For six days you shall labour and do all your work, but the seventh day is a Sabbath for Yahweh your God.'[22] The carrying out of many activities on the Sabbath day was

---

[18] Luke 17:11–19.
[19] John 4:53.
[20] Genesis 2:2–3.
[21] Exodus 16:22–30.
[22] Exodus 20:8–10.

directly prohibited under Jewish law. This included not only a prohibition on all work, but also a prohibition on many mundane tasks such as lighting fires, travelling over a certain distance and carrying items in public.[23]

Thus by carrying his mat in the public place of Bethesda, the now healed man contravenes the law of the Sabbath and brings himself into direct conflict with the Jewish authorities. How does he react to this test of faith? Does he act with a new courage? As we shall see, in the sixth sign the young man whose sight is restored finds courage to confront the Jewish authorities directly. In contrast, here at Bethesda what we learn from the story is that, when the Jewish authorities confront the healed man and reprimand him for carrying his sleeping mat on the Sabbath, his reaction is to blame Jesus for his act. He is all too quick to divert attention away from himself and towards Jesus: 'But the man who cured me told me, "Pick up your sleeping-mat and walk around." '[24] It is worth noting, however, that at this point in the narrative we are told that the man does not know who Jesus is and so is unable to tell the Jews that it was Jesus who had cured him.

When he meets Jesus a second time, later in the temple, and Jesus tells him, 'Now you are well again, do not sin any more, or something worse may happen to you,'[25] the man's immediate reaction is to go back to the Jewish authorities and tell them that it was, in fact, Jesus who cured him. In so doing, he must have known that this would cause those same authorities to condemn Jesus. Whether this is done out of fear, or out of an attempt to

---

[23] For a much fuller explanation of Jewish law and tradition at the time of Jesus, see Stephen M. Wylen, *The Jews in the Time of Jesus* (Paulist Press International, 1995).
[24] John 5:11.
[25] John 5:14.

win favour, we do not know. What we are certain of, however, is that there is absolutely no evidence that through his healing the sick man has had a change of heart or a redirection of his life. There is no sign of any conversion. And, without a doubt, the man's actions of reporting Jesus to the Jewish authorities contribute to the chain of events that will eventually lead Jesus to the cross at Golgotha.

This man's meeting with Jesus, then, is very different from what has gone on before at Cana. But from this encounter we can learn much. Even after our own personal encounter with Jesus it is unlikely that we will have been instantly transformed into a wonderful and better person. What is true is that our first faith encounter with Jesus is only the beginning of our journey in faith and that it is dependent upon us attempting to have an open and receiving heart. At Bethesda the man may have been physically healed, but the real healing, the healing of his heart, had not occurred. This was not because Jesus wished to deny him this healing – indeed, Jesus did not deny him the gift of physical healing either – but because the man's alienation had become so great that he could not open his heart to Christ. Nevertheless, it is in the healing of the heart that the true wonder of the Lord's grace can be found.

I have travelled to Lourdes and it is wonderful and truly humbling to witness the joy and faith of so many, in the midst of such pain and suffering, as pilgrims from all over the world come seeking a new miraculous sign from God. While many come seeking the sign of a physical healing, one of the most powerful signs of the Kingdom that I witnessed there was the emotional healing of a woman. For over twenty years she had held in her heart a grain of hate for the doctor she blamed for the premature death of her father. That grain of hatred had begun as no more than the size of a small speck of dust, but had now become like a stone, weighing her down, pulling her into a place of bitterness and anger. The true miracle of Lourdes was to witness her let go of that stone and say of that doctor, 'I forgive him.'

At various points in our lives we will find ourselves like the sick man at Bethesda, our hearts closed and alienated from the God of love. Certainly, through the joy of baptism and the sacraments and the love of community, we have encountered Jesus, but that does not mean that our hearts are always open to him and the healing that he offers. Our hearts at different times in our journey may be like the different soils which Mark describes in the parable of the sower.[26] We would, perhaps, like to think that our hearts are always like the rich soil, in which the seed of God's love can be planted and grow and produce a good crop. However, often the reality is very different. The soil of our hearts may be like that found near to the path, hard and impenetrable, where the seed of God's love is sown but cannot take root and is eaten by birds; or the soil of our heart may be like the rocky road where the seed of love initially springs up like a sapling but because there is no depth of soil, it cannot survive the scorching sun as it lacks deep and sustaining roots; or perhaps there is no soil at all and the seed of love is sown but is choked by thorns.[27]

The truth of the matter is that we are not born or baptised saints and in our lives we will have moments when we close ourselves off from God. Nevertheless, that does

---

[26] Mark 4.
[27] Mark 4:4–7.

not mean that God cannot turn those moments into an occasion that gives glory to him. Thus in the healing of the man at Bethesda, we see a sign of the Kingdom. In David's pursuit of Bathsheba and his attempts to cover up his adultery, attempts which ultimately lead to the murder of her husband Uriah the Hittite, we see a king's repentance and turning back to God.[28] Indeed, Adrian Graffy writes of the Davidic tradition:

> The history of the early years of the dynasty of David presents events to challenge faith in the God who chose such a man and such a family. But the honesty of the tradition is even more striking. It seems to be affirming that God chooses weak human beings despite their weakness.[29]

Similarly, in Peter's threefold denial of Jesus,[30] we also witness his threefold affirmation of love to the risen Jesus,[31] and in that affirmation lies the beginning of a journey to Rome which will end in his own personal Golgotha and martyrdom, giving glory to God. Equally, in our own struggles in faith and our inevitable failures, we should not see an insincere sinner but a genuine pilgrim – one seeking time and again to do better, but always reaching out to the healing love of God.

Yes, our witness to Christ may be based on many occasions on stony ground, but that does not mean that we are denied God's mercy and healing. Nor should it mean that we deny ourselves forgiveness and so alienate ourselves from God and from those around us. We must learn to be gentle with ourselves, to treat ourselves with

---

[28] 2 Samuel 11-12.
[29] Adrian Graffy, *Alive and Active: The Old Testament beyond 2000* (The Columbia Press, 1999).
[30] John 18:17, 25-27.
[31] John 21:15-17.

understanding and mercy. For in accepting our own weakness and faults, we will be able to reach out to those we find difficult, those we find too easy to judge. In this truth, we will find it easier to be gentle not only with ourselves, but with each other. Archbishop Rowan Williams tells the story of Abba Moses, one of the most famous of the Desert Fathers, who when asked to judge a brother who had committed a fault, set off taking a leaking jug full of water with him:

'The others came out to meet him and said, 'What is this, Father?' The old man said to them, 'My sins run out behind me and I cannot see them, yet here I am coming to sit in judgment on the mistakes of somebody else.' When they heard this, they called off the meeting.'[32]

By remembering and being conscious of our own weaknesses, our own imperfections and our own vulnerability, we can recognise in the unlovable the causes of their own pain and sufferings. We can begin to recognise in them the same pain and suffering that we experience. In that recognition, we shall begin to find and experience an empathy, a solidarity, a fellowship and a compassion which we have never seen or felt before. And in that recognition we shall cease to see the faces of those we find difficult, the faces of the alienated and the unlovable, but rather we will see the faces of our own brothers and sisters in Christ.

At the 'House of Mercy' Jesus shows us how to reach beyond ourselves, how to move beyond the 'I' of our lives to the 'you' of community. This is the essence of true mercy. This is a tall order, and certainly in its living

---

[32] Rowan Williams, *Silence and Honey Cakes - The Wisdom of the Desert* (Lion Hudson, 2003).

practice often seems close to a utopian dream. Although this way of living may be counterintuitive to the dictates of the secular world, this is the challenge to which the story at Bethesda directs us, a challenge that Jesus himself made to the Jewish authorities by the healing of the sick man on the Sabbath.

People of the new Sabbath

How do we as a Church respond to the challenge of Bethesda? Let us turn now to the final part of the story. As we have learnt, upon his healing, the Jews immediately ask the man who cured him. The man replies that he does not know. However, upon meeting Jesus again and learning his identity, he goes back to the Jewish authorities to tell them that it was Jesus. We then learn two startling things about their reaction. First, they begin to harass Jesus because he healed the man on the Sabbath. Second, when Jesus defends his actions, answering their charges by saying, 'My Father still goes on working [on the Sabbath], and I am at work, too,'[33] they become so incensed that they are 'even more intent on killing him'.[34] There is, therefore, a clear implication that their murderous intent had begun to be formulated even before Jesus spoke of God as his own Father or claimed equality with him. We shall see this intent reach its culmination in the aftermath of the seventh sign, the raising of Lazarus.

It was the act of healing a man on the Sabbath that gave the Jewish authorities enough reason not only to harass

---

[33] John 5:17.
[34] John 5:18.

Jesus, but also to start upon a plan to kill him. As we have seen, the Sabbath was held to be holy and sacred. The observance of the Sabbath, and the command to keep it holy, came from the mouth of God himself and, because of this command, the Jewish people had built up a complicated system of laws and religious observances.

For Jesus to heal a man on the Sabbath was not only a contravention of Jewish law, but a revolutionary and radical act that was inevitably going to bring him into confrontation with the Jewish authorities and lead to his death. Such an act challenged not only their theological view of the world, but also the very basis on which the Jewish hierarchy founded their authority – a fact Jesus would certainly have known.

By curing the man on the Sabbath, Jesus deliberately set himself against the Jewish authorities and showed that his Kingdom was radically different from – and incompatible with – the worldview and theological values held by the Jewish people at that time. He healed on the Sabbath. It is, therefore, little wonder that the Jewish people were so angered that they immediately began to plot to kill Jesus. Radical Kingdom values will always face opposition, sometimes even violent opposition.

It was such opposition to Kingdom values that led to the martyrdom of St Thomas More at the hands of King Henry VIII. It was opposition to Kingdom values that led to the death of Saint Maximilian Kolbe in the gas chambers at Auschwitz. And it was opposition to Kingdom values that led to the assassination of Archbishop Oscar Romero as he celebrated Mass in the cathedral church of San Salvador on 24 March 1980.

In his act of healing the man at Bethesda on the Sabbath, Jesus rejects the old ways of the Sabbath and commits a new and radical Sabbath act, one which threatens the very society in which he finds himself. He challenges the old law and ways of being with a new, radical view of the world and of his Father. By his example he calls us to be people of the new Sabbath.

So, as we come together as the Church, the community of Jesus, how radical and life-changing do we allow our Sabbath act to be? Do we, like Jesus, with deliberation set our face against the authorities of today when their values do not accord to the values of God's Kingdom? Can we hear the voice of the Church, standing firm, calling all to the new Kingdom? Or do we, as a community, retreat into the Church, into ritual and self-centred personal belief, hiding behind our church doors hoping that we will be unnoticed and that no one will knock upon them? This is the challenge which Jesus sets before all women and men who would follow him.

For many of us, church can become a safe and unchallenging place, a place where we are reaffirmed in our own beliefs and ways of thinking, and where we seek out only those who share and agree with our view of the world and God. It can also appear to be a daunting, cold and unwelcoming place to those who walk by but never cross its steps. It is easy for our experience of church to become exclusive through force of habit. We should never allow this to happen: church should be a place where we are constantly challenged. And as a Church we should be a community where we constantly challenge all to respond to the call of Christ. How radical would our Sabbath act be if we were to celebrate our Eucharist not behind the closed doors of a church, but in a crowded Sunday shopping centre, behind the barred gates of our prisons, or among the poor, lonely and homeless of our towns?

At Bethesda we learn that at the heart of God's Kingdom is a requirement to reach out to the alienated, to go beyond ourselves even in the face of opposition. This means that, as a Church, we must reach out beyond our walls to the alone and the 'unchurched', to those whom we will not find in our church pews on a Sunday. This is, and must be, our radical Sabbath act. Like Jesus, we must have the courage as a Church to offer a new, radical way. We must be true people of the Sabbath.

Where can we find the strength to challenge the very foundations of the world in which we live? What is the nature of our mission? How are we to act as channels of the challenger God's disturbing love? Surely this is too much to ask?

The answers to all these questions are to be found in the fourth of John's signs. And, surprisingly, we shall find those answers in five simple loaves of barley bread.

4

'But what is that among so many?'

The miracles of the loaves (John 6:1-15)

In the third sign Jesus' call to us is to reach beyond ourselves to those who are alienated and alone, to those who
are outside the camp. Now we turn to the fourth of the
seven signs, the miracle of the loaves and the feeding of
the multitude. Let us first remind ourselves of the story
John tells.[1]

We are told that following the events of Bethesda, Jesus
crossed the Sea of Galilee followed by a large crowd who
had been impressed by the signs he had made in curing the
sick. Then he climbed a hillside and sat down with his
disciples. John tells us that, seeing the crowd, Jesus was
concerned that the people had nothing to eat, so he asked
Philip where they could buy some bread to feed them.
Philip responded that the two hundred denarii they held in
the communal purse would only be enough to give each of
the multitude a little to eat. Andrew, the brother of Simon
Peter, pointed out to Jesus a small child who had five

---

[1] John 6:1-15.

barley loaves and two fish. On seeing this, Jesus instructed the disciples to make the people sit down on the grassy hillside.

He then took the bread and the fish, gave thanks, and distributed it to all who were there; they all had as much as they wanted. When they had finished eating, Jesus instructed the disciples to pick up the pieces that were left so that nothing would be wasted. On picking up the left-over scraps from the five barley loaves there was enough to fill twelve baskets. On seeing the sign, the people declared that Jesus must be the prophet who had come into the world. Realising that they were about to take him and make him king, Jesus fled back to the hills alone.

How, then, does the sign challenge us today? As with all the signs we have encountered thus far, its true wonder lies perhaps not so much in its physical nature – the feeding of the multitude – as in what it reveals about the nature of Jesus. This sign is not unique to John; all three of the Synoptic Gospels also contain details of the feeding of the multitude. But in John's narrative we shall see that Jesus directs us through his actions to the threefold royal, prophetic and priestly elements of mission and, in so doing, the challenger God invites us, too, to share in that ministry with him. Strangely, as we shall see, central to these signposts are the five loaves of barley.

Five barley loaves and the nature of mission

All four of the Gospels relate the story of the feeding of the multitude. However, it is only in John's telling that the specific nature of the type of bread that the little boy offers is brought to the fore. John is very careful to describe the bread as being made from barley. Why is this of relevance? Is this a level of detail that was just left out of the other three Gospels, or does its particular and specific inclusion by John reveal some deeper significance?

In Jewish society at that time barley was used to feed livestock, hence bread made from barley was thought of as food for the poor. However, for the Jewish people the reference to barley and bread would not have been lost. It would have called to mind two very specific stories from Scripture: those of Ruth and Elisha. Moreover, Jesus' act of giving thanks to God for the bread would have had a striking resemblance to the priest-king Melchizedek. If we examine each of these stories in turn, we will discover that they speak to us of the threefold kingly, prophetic and priestly mission which we are each called to live out through the waters of our own baptism.

Ruth: faithfulness, redemption and the royal mission

At the end of the narrative of the fourth sign, John tells us that Jesus, realising that the Jewish people might seize him and make him king, fled alone to the hills. What, then, was so special about this sign, the feeding of five thousand, that it would have given the Jewish people the notion that Jesus was the promised Messiah, a king in David's line, the anointed one, the Christ? In the story of Ruth we will, perhaps, find part of the answer.

Weaving their way through the narrative of Ruth are numerous references to barley and bread. In fact, one can argue that without barley the whole story of Ruth, and hence the Davidic dynasty, may have ended very differently. Ruth was not a Jew but a Moabite, who, after the

81

death of Naomi's husband Elimelech, married one of her two sons. However, on the death of both of Naomi's sons, and with no male members of the family left to care for them, Naomi instructed both her daughters-in-law to return to their own families. Ruth, however, refused to leave Naomi, declaring, 'Do not press me to leave you and to stop going with you, for wherever you go, I shall go, wherever you live, I shall live. Your people will be my people, and your God will be my God.'[2]

We immediately witness Ruth not only as a woman of faith, but also as a woman who, through an act of self-sacrifice, is prepared to demonstrate her loyalty. We witness a woman who is prepared to forgo her own family and beliefs to stay with Naomi and to commit to Naomi's God for the sake of her mother-in-law.

Thus Naomi, accompanied by Ruth, returned to her home in Bethlehem – 'the house of bread' – where she arrived at the beginning of the barley harvest. There, Ruth set off to find work and came to a plot of land belonging to Boaz, a kinsman of Naomi. She asked Boaz to let her pick up the scraps of barley that the harvesters left behind. Boaz gave her permission and told her that, because he had heard of what she had done for Naomi, he had instructed that she be kept safe, protected and given water. 'May Yahweh repay you for what you have done, and may you be richly rewarded by Yahweh.'[3] Boaz then made a heap of barley grain for her to eat and she 'ate till her hunger was satisfied, and she had some left over.'[4]

On hearing this news Naomi told Ruth that Boaz had a 'right of redemption' over her. Under Jewish law, the right

[2] Ruth 1:16.
[3] Ruth 2:12.
[4] Ruth 2:14.

of redemption existed where a brother, or in default of a brother another male kinsman, could take and marry the brother's widow to preserve his inheritance and family lineage.[5] Naomi instructed Ruth to offer herself to Boaz and to do whatever he told her. So that night, Ruth lay down at Boaz's feet beside a pile of barley.

On seeing Ruth, Boaz again blessed her: ' "May Yahweh bless you, daughter," he said, "for this second act of faithful love of yours is greater than the first, since you have not run after young men, poor or rich." '[6] However, Boaz told Ruth that he would exercise his right of redemption over her only if another kinsman, who had a prior right of redemption, refused to claim it. When that relative declined to exercise his right, faithful to his word, Boaz took Ruth as his wife and they bore a son, Obed. Obed was the father of Jesse, who in turn was the father of David. And so, through Ruth's faithfulness and sacrifice, and Boaz's act of redemption, the lineage of the future King David was secured.

As we can see, the numerous references to barley and bread in the story of Ruth are striking. They are woven through Ruth's narrative and are integral to her story. From the return to Bethlehem, 'the house of bread', to her collecting the leftover scraps of barley at harvest time; from eating the scraps of barley until she was satisfied, with some still left over, to offering herself to Boaz on the threshing floor beside a pile of barley: all these events ultimately lead to and bring about the kingship of David. One might go so far as to argue that there would be no

---

[5] Deuteronomy 25:5–6: 'Her husband's brother must come to her and, exercising his duty as brother, make her his wife, and the first son she bears must assume the dead brother's name; by this means his name will not be obliterated from Israel.'

[6] Ruth 3:10.

king were it not for the accompanying barley events in the life of Ruth. Taken in isolation, it may be argued that the link between the barley loaves and the story of Ruth, and hence the kingship of Jesus, is tenuous. However, as we shall see, if it is coupled to the remembrance of the priest-king Melchizedek, John is clearly directing us to the kingship of Jesus.

In Jesus' act of breaking and distributing the five loaves of bread made from barley, we are reminded of the story of Ruth, a story of faithfulness and redemption which eventually leads to the anointing and kingship of David. And in bringing forth the story of Ruth, John also points us to the kingship of Jesus. It is, therefore, unsurprising that the narrative of the story ends with Jesus fleeing lest the Jewish people seize him and make him king. Jesus is the anointed one, the promised and long-awaited Messiah, and the mission to which he is called, and to which he also calls us, is a royal one. We will explore these themes further, but it is sufficient to note for now that by reminding us of the story of Ruth, John begins to reveal to us the true nature of who Jesus is, his true kingship.

Elisha: the prophetic mission

John also tells us of another strong reaction by the witnesses to the sign. 'Seeing the sign that he had done, the people said, "This is indeed the prophet who is to come into the world."'[7] What was it that caused such a strong reaction? Again the answer is to be found in the Jewish Scriptures. The witnesses to the sign would have been

[7] John 6:14.

directly reminded of the story of Elisha. Elisha was the attendant to the great prophet Elijah, but when Elijah was taken up to heaven, Elisha assumed his prophetic role. Indeed, he received from Elijah, at his own request, a double portion of the prophet's spirit,[8] and went on to perform many signs. Amongst these, the feeding of one hundred soldiers in Gilgai during a time of famine in the country bears a striking resemblance to Jesus' feeding of the five thousand.

> A man came from Baal-Shalishah, bringing the man of God bread from the first-fruits, twenty barley loaves and fresh grain still in the husk. 'Give it to the company to eat,' Elisha said. But his servant replied, 'How can I serve this to a hundred men?' 'Give it to the company to eat,' he insisted, 'for Yahweh says this, "They will eat and have some left over."' He served them; they ate and had some left over, as Yahweh had said.[9]

The similarities between Jesus' sign and Elisha's miracle are striking, although it is clear that Jesus' sign is on a far grander scale. Jesus feeds a multitude of five thousand with five barley loaves and fish. On Elisha's instructions the one hundred soldiers are fed with twenty barley loaves. In both cases there is some bread left over, and in the case of Jesus it is enough to fill twelve baskets. Elisha is faced with the doubt of his servant: 'How can I serve this to a hundred men?' Jesus faces the doubt of Philip and Andrew. Philip protests that the two hundred denarii they have will buy only enough bread to give each person a tiny piece. Andrew, too, although bringing the small boy with the five

---

[8] 2 Kings 2:9.
[9] 2 Kings 4:42–44.

loaves and two fish to Jesus' attention, declares, 'But what is that among so many?'[10]

In witnessing the sign, it is inconceivable that the Jewish people would have failed to recognise a far grander sign than that of the prophet Elisha. If Jesus could perform such a sign, far greater than Elisha who, after all, had received a double portion of the spirit of Elijah, then perhaps Jesus was as great as, if not greater than, Elijah? Perhaps Jesus was even Elijah returned from heaven? The five thousand cannot have failed to recognise in the sign the act of a great and wondrous prophet of God. They would not only have seen in Jesus a great prophet, but also would have observed his prophetic mission in action. We shall return to this theme later.

Melchizedek: the priestly mission

We have already seen that the witnesses to the sign would have recognised great truths about the nature of Jesus' kingly and prophetic identity and mission. John further directs us to an equally great truth regarding Jesus' priestly identity and mission.

John narrates that, before distributing the bread and fish, Jesus tells the people to sit down and then he gives thanks. All three Synoptic Gospels give far greater and consistent details of what Jesus did in giving thanks. Indeed, Matthew, Mark and Luke all use identical language to tell us that when Jesus took the five loaves and two fish, he 'raised his eyes to heaven and said the blessing'.[11] The consistency of

---

[10] John 6:9.
[11] Matthew 14:19; Mark 6:41; Luke 9:16.

Matthew, Mark and Luke means that it is highly likely that John's concise description, Jesus 'gave thanks',[12] is simply that: a shorthand description of Jesus blessing the bread and the fish.

This act of blessing would also have drawn the witnesses to the story of another king from the Jewish Scriptures, that of Melchizedek. Although little is known about him, we do know that he was a king and a priest who probably gave rise to a priestly order. Indeed, in Psalm 110 we find the description of King David as 'a priest for ever of the order of Melchizedek'.[13] What would have reminded the Jewish people of Melchizedek, however, was Jesus' act of blessing the bread. In the book of Genesis we learn that Melchizedek comes out to meet Abram on Abram's return from defeating Chedor-Laomer and makes an offering of bread and wine. 'Melchizedek king of Salem brought bread and wine; he was a priest of God Most High. He pronounced this blessing: "Blessed be Abram by God Most High, Creator of heaven and earth. And blessed be God Most High for putting your enemies into your clutches."'[14]

What is unusual about this episode is that Melchizedek offers a sacrifice of bread and wine rather than an animal. At that time it was a custom throughout the known world that animals be sacrificed as an offering to God, or whichever deities were worshipped, in place of the person who was making the offering or for whom the offering was made. In this regard it was commonplace for birds, goats and lambs to be sacrificed.[15]

---

[12] John 6:11.
[13] Psalm 110:4.
[14] Genesis 14:18–19.
[15] For a fuller description of sacrifice rites in the Old Testament, see Scott Hahn, *The Lamb's Supper* (Doubleday, 1999).

However, for the Jewish people, the offering of sacrifice meant much more. It was a sign of the promise, a sign of the covenant that God had made with them. It was after the floodwaters had subsided that Noah built an altar and made a burnt offering of birds to Yahweh. In response, Yahweh makes a covenant with Noah and with his descendants that never again will the world and its inhabitants be destroyed by a flood.[16] Similarly Abraham, when spared by Yahweh from sacrificing his son Isaac, instead makes a sacrifice of a young ram which Yahweh provides. In return for his willingness to have sacrificed his son, Yahweh once again reasserts his covenant with Abraham: 'I will shower blessings on you and make your descendants as numerous as the stars of heaven and the grains of sand on the seashore.'[17] Finally, the Passover lamb is slaughtered as an offering and as a sign to God, and through that sign the Jewish people are spared from the death of their firstborn. This act ultimately leads to their liberation from Egypt.[18]

But Melchizedek's offering is not of a bird, a ram or a lamb. It is an offering of bread and wine. In it we can perhaps see the foretelling of our own Eucharistic offering. Indeed, in the Catholic tradition, Melchizedek is expressly referenced in the first Eucharistic prayer. And in raising his eyes to heaven, giving thanks and blessing the bread, we witness in Jesus the priestly role of offering a sacrifice to his Father in heaven and interceding on our behalf. We also witness in Jesus' sacrifice, the breaking and sharing of the bread among the multitude, the foretelling of the ultimate surrender he will make of his life as our new Passover lamb in his violent death on the cross. It is hardly a

[16] Genesis 9:11.
[17] Genesis 22:17.
[18] Exodus 12.

coincidence that the sign of the feeding of the multitude took place when the feast of the Jewish Passover was so near. We shall return to this fact later, when we explore the fifth sign of Jesus walking on the water.

Sharing in the royal, prophetic and priestly ministry of Jesus

In the story of the feeding of the five thousand, we have learnt yet again that if we go beyond the simple narrative, beyond the physical wonder of the sign, we discover something truly wonderful about the nature and identity of Jesus. Here we see Jesus as king, prophet and priest. However, we must respond to the Gospel. We cannot be passive. What is Jesus calling us to do through the wonder of the sign?

At the heart of the sign is the central meaning of sacrificial sharing. Philip is prepared to share the communal purse to buy bread for the multitude, but he realises that this is not going to buy enough bread for everyone to be fed. It is through the sacrifice, sharing and gift of the small boy that Jesus receives the five loaves and the fish which will feed the multitude. And it is through the sacrifice of prayer and the sharing of the bread and fish by Jesus that the five thousand are fed. If we are to learn anything from the story it is that we, too, must weave the narrative of Jesus' sacrifice and sharing into every aspect of our lives. In short, we are called through our baptism to share in Jesus' sacrificial ministry. This ministry is simultaneously royal, prophetic and priestly in nature. But what does this mean in practice?

A royal ministry

We have already seen, in the healing of the sick man on the Sabbath at Bethesda, that Jesus' kingly or Kingdom values were, and are, completely different from those of the world. As Jesus himself said before Pilate, 'Mine is not a kingdom of this world.'[19] Jesus' Kingdom values are radical and challenging. At their core we do not find a morality or ethical code founded on the quest for earthly, political or military power. Nor are these values founded on a search for wealth and comfort. Rather, the ethical code to which we are called to abide by as Christians has at its heart a call to remind us who we are: the sons and daughters of the Father.

Jesus' values are founded on an identification with, and a reaching out to, the poor, the orphaned, the widowed, the dispossessed and the alienated in our society, no matter how unlovable or difficult we may find them, in our limited capacity to love. It is a mission to reach out to those outside the camp. It follows, then, that since Jesus' Kingdom values are so radical and contrast so strongly with those of the world, to share in Jesus' royal ministry is to share in something very different from anything we can judge by the world's values. When we share in the royal ministry of Jesus, when we come together as a royal Church, our values and our behaviour must be aligned to Jesus' Kingdom values. Jesus' model of kingship is one which is firmly founded on concern for others and, out of that concern, service to others. This is a model of kingship where all are provided for and all are welcomed.

John tells us that Jesus crossed the Sea of Galilee. We

---

[19] John 18:36.

know that the Passover was near and perhaps he wanted to be alone with his disciples to prepare for the feast. Yet the crowds followed Jesus – not because they were aligned to his Kingdom values, but because they hoped to see another sign. We are reminded of the words that Jesus spoke to the royal official in the second sign, 'Unless you see signs and portents you will not believe.'[20] Jesus may well have wanted to be left alone to find peace and solitude so close to the Passover. Yet on seeing the crowd, he does not rebuke them, nor does he try to leave. His first and only concern is the welfare of the multitude. It is because of this that he asks Philip where they can buy some bread to feed them. We see here, in this action, a loving, caring God, a royal king whose concerns for the poor are at the forefront of his thoughts. In the sign Jesus shows us that integral to the royal mission is a concern always for others.

Next, Jesus asks the crowd sit down at a spot where, we are told, there is plenty of grass. In the dusty, sandy region of Israel, grass was a sign of abundance, which again gives us a further clue to the nature of Jesus' kingship. We are instantly reminded of the image of God as the good shepherd: 'Yahweh is my shepherd, I lack nothing. In grassy meadows he lets me lie.'[21]

The royal mission in which we share is akin to the task of a good shepherd, whose concern must always be to look after others' needs rather than his own. It is a concern that must not be expressed simply in platitudes, but must be followed by action.

Nowhere is this royal ministry better demonstrated than

---

[20] John 4:48.
[21] Psalm 23:1-2.

in Jesus' radical Sabbath act of washing the disciples' feet on the night before his death and crucifixion. This was definitely not an act of royalty as we would understand it today. It was an act of servitude. In Jerusalem at that time, the task of washing the feet of the household and its guests would have been delegated to the lowest of the servants. Richard Bauckham writes:

> Washing someone else's feet was an unpleasant task, which no one except a servant or a slave could be expected to do. So menial a task was it that in a household with a hierarchy of slaves and servants, it would be the duty of the slaves, not of the servants who performed less demeaning tasks such as waiting at table. It was, in fact, the quintessentially servile task, the one thing that no one else would do.[22]

At the Last Supper, therefore, Jesus' act shocked his disciples because it turned over the pre-existing social order. Jesus became a slave to his disciples. Peter was adamant in his opposition to this act: ' "Never!" said Peter. "You shall never wash my feet." '[23] It was only when Jesus told Peter that unless he allowed him to do so he could have no share of him that Peter gave in. And why did Jesus do this? His answer is direct: 'I have given you an example so that you may copy what I have done to you. In all truth I tell you, no servant is greater than his master, no messenger is greater than the one who sent him.'[24]

Jesus cannot be any clearer: both individually, and collectively as the Church of Christ, we are called to share in the royal ministry. Thus, when we fight for economic

---

[22] Richard Bauckham, *The Testimony of the Beloved Disciple* (Baker Academic, 2007).
[23] John 13:8.
[24] John 13:15–16.

justice for the poor in our communities and in the world, we share in this royal ministry. When we open the doors of our churches and schools to those seeking refuge from unjust regimes, we share in this royal ministry. And when we open the doors of our homes to the homeless, we share in this royal ministry.

However, when we seek our own advancement over that of others out of pride and ego, we oppose Jesus' royal Kingdom values. When we have no regard for the unjust genesis of the consumer products we buy, often produced in almost slave-like conditions in the third world, we oppose Jesus' royal Kingdom values. And when we discriminate against each other on grounds of race, gender or sexual orientation, we oppose Jesus' royal Kingdom values.

In all of our personal, relational and commercial dealings, and in every aspect of our lives, we must be mindful of the image of the Servant King bending low to wash the feet of his disciples and the words he speaks: 'I have given you an example so that you may copy what I have done to you.'[25]

There is one other aspect of the royal mission we should dwell upon, and that is derived from the heroic nature of kingship. History and legend focus our minds upon the heroic exploits of kings. Whether it be brave King Leonidas, against all odds defending Sparta from the hordes of Persia at Thermopylae, or King Henry, leading the English army into battle against the French at Agincourt, we are never left in doubt about the heroic virtue and nature of kingship, where a king is always prepared to lay down his life in defence of his kingdom and his people.

---

[25] John 13:15.

This is no less so in the case of Jesus. We see this same heroism in the action of the little boy who comes forward to present his meagre offering of loaves and fishes so that all may be fed. And in Jesus' act of breaking the bread and sharing it among the five thousand, we witness the fore-telling of his own body being broken and torn on the cross at Golgotha, for the sake of his Kingdom and his beloved people.

As is so often the case, it is the women of the Church who demonstrate this true heroism. Jean Donovan was a lay missionary working with the Maryknoll order in El Salvador in the early 1980s. It was a time when a cruel dictatorship ruled El Salvador and death squads freely roamed the streets. It was under this regime that Arch-bishop Romero of San Salvador was assassinated while saying Mass.

One evening, while driving back from the airport, Jean Donovan and three nuns, Dorothy Kazel, Maura Clarke and Ita Ford, were stopped at gunpoint by undercover National Guardsmen. They were raped and murdered and their bodies unceremoniously dumped in a shallow grave. Their deaths helped change public opinion in the United States, which had hitherto supported such an unjust and cruel regime. Shortly before she died, Jean, showing her true royal heroism in Christ, wrote:

The Peace Corps left today and my heart sank low. The danger is extreme and they were right to leave ... Now I must assess my own position, because I am not up for suicide. Several times I have decided to leave El Salvador. I almost could, except for the children, the poor, bruised victims of this insanity. Who would care for them? Whose heart could be so staunch as to favor the reasonable thing in a sea of their tears and loneliness? Not mine, dear friend, not mine.[26]

In partaking in the royal mission of Jesus, we, as the community of Jesus, are ultimately called upon to share in the heroism of Christ, to put fear behind us and to walk with Jesus in the way of the cross. Nowhere is this heroism more required than in the exercise of the prophetic ministry.

A prophetic ministry

What must we do to share in the prophetic ministry of Jesus? The role of the prophet is not to make wild predictions of what may or may not happen in the future. The role of the biblical prophet has always been to call people back to a right relationship with God. Adrian Graffy writes:

> a prophet is one who is able to hear the word, and has the courage to proclaim what he hears. The prophet's lot is not a happy one, for the message will frequently fall upon deaf ears.[27]

Thus there are two essential elements to true prophetic ministry. The first is having the ability to listen to the word of God. The second is having the courage, the heroic courage, to pass that word on to others even when they do not wish to hear it.

How then, is it possible, in our often frantic and busy lives, to listen to the word of God? First, we must learn to

---

[26] John Dear, *The Life and Example of Jean Donovan* (CommonDreams.org, 2005).
[27] Adrian Graffy, *Alive and Active: The Old Testament Beyond 2000* (The Columbia Press, 1999).

rise above the clamour of the world. Our lives are full of noise. There is not a part of the world where at some point during the day the sound of conflict cannot be heard. Whether it be between tribal nations fighting with each other, or in our own inner cities and communities where the sound of gunfire accompanies the tragic taking of young lives.

We spend much of our lives surrounded by what may seem to be a wall of noise. On our daily commute to work, the roar of traffic or the thunder of planes flying overhead crash into our thoughts and private space. Worse still, we become desensitised to the clamour around us. We block out all sounds and become imprisoned in our thoughts, oblivious to the racket around us, when sometimes it is within that very noise that there is hidden a cry for help. We have become a communication society, so that even on those rare occasions when we find ourselves in relative peace, our inner quiet is interrupted. We carry telephones which constantly ring, and the incessant tapping of keys on our mobile devices fills us with the internal clatter of emails or text messages received or sent. If we live in the city it may seem almost impossible to find a place where we can quieten the external and internal noise, where we can allow ourselves to be still enough to listen truly with an open heart and mind.

Not all the sound around us, however, is negative. Much can be good. In our homes we may be assailed by the joyful laughter of our children as they play; the mistuned practice of the clarinet or piano; the raucous chatter of good conversation over a meal shared with cherished family and friends. Nevertheless, it is rare that we spend time in purposeful quiet, a time spent in silence listening for the still small voice of God.

The truth is that many of us, individually and as communities, have forgotten how to be quiet. We have forgotten how to listen. How often, after a busy day at our place of work or looking after the children, do we make the conscious decision just to be quiet? Sadly, it is far easier to reach for the television remote. How often does our local faith community come together just in silence to listen? Indeed, we can too often be tempted to fill our liturgy with so much music and symbolic action that we do not leave space for God to speak to us in and through the silence. The best conversationalists are those who say the least and listen the most. The most faithful and action-driven Christian communities are always those that spend time collectively, in the stillness of quiet, listening to and discerning the word of God.

The first thing we must do, both individually and collectively as Church, is to find that quiet time, that sacred space – that time and space which Dom Christopher Jamison, the then Abbot of Worth Abbey, described as 'sanctuary'.[28] Only when we make time to do this can we find what the prophet Elijah heard: the still small voice of God.[29] And in allowing our ears to become attuned to the word of God, we may find that we begin to hear that still small voice of God speaking to us not only in the quiet, but also in and through the noise of our daily lives.

The second element of sharing in the prophetic ministry is having the courage to proclaim the heard and discerned word of God. As we have already seen, both in the story of Elisha feeding the one hundred soldiers and in Jesus' feeding of the five thousand, there were those who had

---

[28] Christopher Jamieson, *Finding Sanctuary: Monastic Steps for Everyday Living* (Orion Books, 2006).
[29] 1 Kings 19:12.

questions. In the case of Elisha it was his servant who doubted: 'How can I serve this to a hundred men?' In the case of Jesus it was Philip and Andrew. The true prophetic voice always speaks in the face of doubt and opposition; it is never silenced.

So how do we exercise the second part of the prophetic ministry? How do we find our prophetic voice? Are we called to stand on a soapbox outside our local super-market, or to stand on Parliament Green shouting out the word of God? For the vast majority of us, thankfully the answer to this will be 'no'. However, we are called to exercise the prophetic voice to call ourselves, our com-munities and society back to a right relationship with God. What does this mean?

First, we must listen to the prophetic voice which is within and directed to ourselves. This is the voice of conscience we hear each time we knowingly stray from the path of the Lord. This is the voice that lovingly calls us back to him when we waver in our commitment or resolve. This is the voice through which Jesus speaks:

> Come back to Yahweh your God
> your guilt was the cause of your downfall.
> Provide yourself with words
> and come back to Yahweh.
> Say to him, 'Take all guilt away
> and give us what is good'.[30]

However, it is not enough simply to listen to that pro-phetic voice within us; we must also act upon it. Where that voice calls us to change direction from a wrongful or addictive path in our lives, then we must try to follow

---

[30] Hosea 14:2-3.

another road. Where that voice calls us to think anew about our neighbour, then we must try to recreate our mindset and cast aside old prejudices and hatreds. And when that voice calls us to heal the broken or difficult relationships in our lives, then we must try to reach out in love, no matter how hard this may be.

Second, collectively as the gathered Church, we must be prepared to listen to the prophetic voices within our own faith community which challenge the way we come together and live and love as the body of the Church. This does not mean that we abandon truth, but it does mean that where the Holy Spirit prompts us, we should be prepared to be open to finding new ways of expressing that truth. Perhaps today this means being prepared to debate and converse openly with each other around often painful and difficult issues. This does not mean we should desert existing Church teaching, but we must be open to the possibility of the ever-creative Holy Spirit constantly asking us to rethink and test the truth of our established positions.

Third, the Church needs to find, now more than ever, a prophetic voice within society advocating the gospel of life which Jesus brings. This needs a Church which is prepared to take action on all levels, and we shall explore this further in our examination of the seventh sign. However, for now, if the Church is to find her true prophetic voice in society, she must first find a voice to which her own faithful will listen. The quality of preaching in many of our parishes is pitifully poor. A far greater emphasis must be placed on the importance of preaching the Word of God in our diocesan priestly and diaconate formation programmes, where candidates must learn to speak to the heart and spirit and not just to the rational mind.

Our own national Church in the United Kingdom needs

to find her prophetic voice. We need a strong, clear and unified voice in local and national politics which is prepared to call our society back to a right relationship with God. This does not mean that the Church should be party political, but it is foolish to think that the Church cannot and should not be political in its engagement with the world. Kingdom values are radical and by their very nature political, in that they challenge and seek to change the existing world order. It was sad to witness the relative silence of the national Church in the immediate aftermath of the riots which took place in August 2011.

Finally, and most importantly, we as the laity cannot escape a role in this part of prophetic ministry. We must be prepared to speak out in every situation, whether at work, in our local communities, or indeed in our own church. In short, we must speak out wherever we see injustice or values being enacted which are contrary to the Kingdom values that have been revealed to us through the Word of God and the teaching of the Church. We must exercise a prophetic and challenging voice in our families, in our local communities and in our society. And we must exercise that prophetic and challenging voice in our Church today. However, in exercising that prophetic voice we must also act in a prophetic manner. In our actions we must become living witnesses to the truth of our words. We must walk humbly with Yahweh, and listen to and act upon the prophetic voice from within – that voice which constantly calls us to change our direction, to be true and faithful to the path that Jesus calls us to follow.

A priestly ministry

In the Jewish tradition, it was the role of the priest to intercede with God on behalf of the people. It was the priest who would offer sacrifice and have access to the inner temple, the holy tabernacle. It was his role to be a bridge between humanity and God. It was through Jesus' death at Golgotha that the writer of Hebrews described his actions as those of 'the high priest of all the blessings which were to come', not through the sacrifice of the blood of animals, but through the sacrifice of his own blood.[31]

Today, in the Catholic tradition, it is the priest who offers on behalf of all the faithful the daily sacrifice of the Eucharist and, in so doing, we re-enter into that very moment of Jesus' sacrifice on the cross. In partaking in the Eucharist we share in the royal priesthood of Christ as we gather round the table of the Eucharist. But we are called to do so much more. So in what other ways are we called to share in this priestly role of sacrifice and intercession?

We are called to be a people of sacrifice, to be a people where all our acts, work and deeds are made as a sacrifice to God. This is about bringing our everyday lives, our everyday moments, our joys and our sorrows, our cele-brations and our times of difficulty to the table of the Lord and, in so doing, offering them to God. Even the most simple of our tasks can be made sacrificial. On a recent visit to Canterbury Cathedral, I saw a man enter in what must have been his lunchtime break from work. He gen-uflected reverently, made the sign of the cross and then

---

[31] Hebrews 9:11-14.

101

got out his newspaper and proceeded to do the crossword. Even this simple moment of leisure time was offered as a sacrifice to God.

The Lord also calls us to be a people of prayer and intercession. In our busy and hectic world it is easy to place a higher value on action. We rightfully admire those who leave home and family to work on international aid projects, or those who work with our troubled youth in inner-city projects, or those who have a vocational call to the teaching or nursing professions. However, we sometimes risk overlooking the true value and power of prayer and intercession.

When I was a young man training for the priesthood, at the end of each term the entire house would be called together for a time of prayerful retreat. On one such retreat, the leader was making the point to us all that those who were called to a life of prayer were not to be considered of any less importance than those called to a life of action in the diocesan priestly ministry. He framed the question thus: 'Are you one of those seminarians who lies awake at night thinking about all that wasted talent tied up in convents up and down the country?' Needless to say, the response he received from a seminary full of only just post-adolescent men was not the one he was expecting! But the point he was trying to make, although perhaps not made well, remains true.

Those who are called to a monastic life, or to an enclosed order, play a vital role not only in the life of the Church, but in the life of the world. Without their constant prayer and intercession we cannot begin to imagine what state the Church, let alone the world, would be in now. However, we are all called to share in that same priestly ministry of prayer and intercession. Think, for a moment,

how different our society would be if we were each to
exchange just ten minutes of television each day for ten
minutes of intercessory prayer. Think, for a moment, how
different *we* would be!

If we are honest with ourselves, we can all find time in
our day that is 'dead time'. In our daily existence we spend
much idle time, when the minutes spin by and we seem to
achieve very little, if anything at all. Whether it be sitting in
traffic, on the bus or tube to work, or waiting for the
microwave to ping as we cook our children's dinner, the
power of intercessory prayer could radically transform
these moments. The power of intercessory prayer could
radically change our lives. It could radically change the
communities and the world in which we live.

In the story of the fourth sign, John draws us into the
royal, prophetic and priestly ministry of Jesus. Not only
are we invited further into the mystery of who Jesus is
and into the nature of his ministry, but we are also challenged to take a share in that very same mission. This is no
small task. It is a call to live a life which is a testimony to a
radical Sabbath act, an act which has at its heart kingly
heroism, prophetic courage and priestly sacrifice. But this
is an act which lies at the very core of our own baptismal
mission.

If we were to leave our analysis of the fourth sign here,
we could be forgiven for thinking that surely this is too
much to ask of any person. Yet the beloved disciple still
has much to show us about how the loving grace of God
can work in our lives, and about how it can give us the
strength to live the life to which we are called through the
promise of our baptism. It is to this loving grace of God
that we must now turn as we look further into the
underlying intimate Eucharistic significance of the feeding

of the multitude. John draws us to this intimate encounter with Jesus through the fifth sign – Jesus walking on the water.

5

'It's me. Don't be afraid'

Jesus comes to his disciples walking on the water
(John 6:16-21)

So we come to the fifth sign: Jesus walking on the water. In
the context of the Gospel of John, this sign merits only one
paragraph, a few words. More importantly, it is squashed
between what perhaps might appear the much greater
fourth sign of the feeding of the multitude[1] and Jesus'
theologically rich 'bread of life' discourse at the synagogue
in Capernaum.[2] Given such scant treatment, it might be
tempting to view the sign on a superficial level – as an
example of Jesus' divine nature, his ability to have total
command over the natural world – and then to move on.
However, when we look deeper at the sign itself, as well as
its particular position in the chronological narrative of the
Gospel of John, we will see that it holds an abundantly rich
and deep significance for us today. In fact, it may be argued
that we cannot fully understand either the fourth sign, the
feeding of the multitude, or the 'bread of life' discourse

---

[1] John 6:1–15.
[2] John 6:22–58.

without firmly placing them both in the context of the fifth sign. Simply put, it speaks to us of our intimate sacramental encounter with Jesus today.

Jesus comes to his disciples walking on the water

John tells us that immediately after the feeding of the multitude, Jesus fled back to the hills alone. He did so because he feared that the assembled multitude would try to make him king. However, by fleeing to the hills he leaves his disciples alone, surrounded by this same excitable crowd. Jesus has worked the crowd up into an excited state, but it is the disciples who are left to deal with them. It is they who are left to answer the questions; questions to which they have no real answers. Is he the king? Is he the prophet? Is he the Messiah? It is as if they have been abandoned by Jesus to the mob.

One can only sympathise with the disciples. They were not men of great learning; neither were they great theologians. It is highly unlikely that they would have studied the Scriptures in the same way that the Pharisees and Jewish authorities would have done. They were simple working men who, after witnessing Jesus' act of feeding the great multitude, were probably left in the same state of bewilderment and confusion as the crowds surrounding them.

It is also likely that they were left in a state of anxiety and fear. We know that this highly animated and expectant gathering did not simply melt away at the end of the day after the feeding of the multitude. Instead, their minds were firmly set on waiting for Jesus to return. In all likelihood they were unaware that Jesus had already fled to the

SIGNS GIVEN THAT WE MIGHT ACT

hills. We know that the multitude waited throughout the night, as John tells us that they were still waiting by the shores of the Sea of Galilee the next morning.[3] Like an excited audience at a rock concert, they wanted an encore and were not going to leave until they got one. The crowd had witnessed a great sign; they wanted more and refused to depart until their demands were satisfied. Gradually, on becoming aware of the absence of Jesus, their unwelcome attention would have turned to the remaining disciples, the followers of Christ.

It is natural that the disciples themselves would want, like Jesus, to escape this crowd, to get away as quickly as possible. And so they wait for nightfall and, in the dark, go down to the shore where they board a boat for Capernaum. This would not have been an easy venture, nor one which could have been undertaken without danger. Remember: not all of these men would have been used to the sea, not all of them were fishermen. In the blackness by the shore they would have been afraid of what might lie ahead and of what the darkness of the night would bring.

Today, even though we are an island nation, with so many of us living in cities or inland we have forgotten the tremendous power of the sea and its capacity to change without warning from stillness to brutality. We have lost our sense of awe and wonder as we gaze out beyond the shore. For many of us, perhaps, the sea brings back memories of happy childhood holidays: playing on the beach with the safe lapping tide at our feet, exploring rock pools and building sandcastles. Yet the sea can be violent and dangerous, and even inland waters can prove

---

[3] John 6:22.

treacherous and claim the lives of the prepared and unprepared alike.

On a recent holiday to Cornwall, my wife and I took our children on a small sailing boat and set off across the Camel estuary between Rock and Padstow. It is where the seemingly placid inland waters of the River Camel meet the powerful waters of the Atlantic Ocean. As we set out, the sun shone and the water looked calm and inviting. Nevertheless, a sudden and unexpected change in wind direction from beyond the hills at the bay at Daymer meant that our small sailing boat, a Cornish Shrimper, began to be suddenly buffeted by waves that seemed to emerge from nowhere. At one point I had to grab my son to prevent him from falling overboard.

Luckily, our experienced captain steered us back to safer waters, but while my son found the episode so funny that he could not stop laughing, the experience reinforced for us the sometimes unpredictable and dangerous nature of the sea. In the United Kingdom alone in 2011, the RNLI were called to launch some 8,905 rescue missions in UK coastal waters, saving over 354 lives.[4]

To take a boat at nightfall, then, without the modern safety and navigational equipment to which we have become accustomed today, would have been a frightening experience for the disciples – especially when we consider that 'the wind was strong, and the sea was getting rough'.[5] Further, for the disciples the only light would have been that of the stars and the moon. Their fear of being left with the baying crowd without Jesus, however, must have far outweighed their fear of such a potentially dangerous

[4] RNLI Annual Operations Statistics, 2011.
[5] John 6:18.

journey. For, the Sea of Galilee 'can be quite treacherous. One moment it is calm, and quiet, then winds rushing down from the mountains can suddenly stir up the waters into dangerous waves.'[6]

Perhaps, too, at the heart of the story we begin to witness their greatest fear: not fear of the sea, but rather the nagging doubt that they had been abandoned by the Jesus whom they had come to know and love. He had left them alone, escaping to the hills without them. Would they ever see him again, or would their lives now be left devoid of his loving presence?

Despite their fear, the disciples continued with their plans and began to row out into the dark, across the tempestuous waters. This would have been an exhausting venture. They were not propelled by the power of the wind filling their sails. John tells us they were rowing and, in all likelihood, they were rowing against the tide and the wind. As the wind and the tide grew ever stronger, the sheer physical effort of every stroke of the oars would have sapped them of their strength. Yet they continued fighting against the sea, fighting against the brutal force of nature, fighting against the darkness. It was then, when they were three or four miles out in the midst of their struggle and in the midst of the darkness of the night, that they encountered Jesus coming towards them, walking on the water.

One of the things that is puzzling about this meeting is how the disciples saw Jesus. Apart from the starlight and the light of the moon, it was pitch black. Further, the wind was roaring and the waves were buffeting their boat. In these circumstances, any experienced mariner would be

---

[6] Jean Vanier, *Drawn into the Mystery of Jesus through the Gospel of John* (Darton, Longman & Todd, 2004).

hard put to see even a few feet ahead. Yet here in the violence of the storm, they clearly saw Jesus. John does not give us an answer to this question, but we can only surmise that there must have been something supranatural about the Jesus they met. His presence was felt by the disciples, notwithstanding the violence and impossibility of their environment. The Jesus they met was working above the level of the natural, cutting through the sheer violence of the storm and the surrounding darkness of the night. He transcended both and because of that the disciples were able to see him.

It is only at this point, upon seeing Jesus, that John tells us they were afraid. It would seem, therefore, that seeing Jesus did not dispel their fear: on the contrary, it brought them into a realisation of their fears. It was only upon encountering Jesus that they realised how vulnerable their position had become, that they saw the dangerous situation into which they had put themselves. It was only upon encountering Jesus that they fully realised their fears of being abandoned by him and being left to the crowd. And so, in the same way as the Sea of Reeds became for the escaping Israelites the very real barrier to their liberation from the slavery of Pharaoh, so the Sea of Galilee for the disciples took on the mantle of the sum of all their fears.

What were those fears? Perhaps they were afraid of the supranatural appearance of Jesus, the ghostly figure approaching them, walking on the water, transcending nature. Or perhaps they were afraid because in some way they felt that they had let Jesus down. Philip and Andrew, perhaps, felt their lack of faith in Jesus' ability to feed the multitude would now be punished. Perhaps Peter felt he had let Jesus down by deserting the multitude. Taken against this backdrop, the encounter of the disciples with the risen Jesus on the shore of Tiberias in the final chapter of the Gospel of John forms a stark contrast and takes on new meaning.[7] For there, after the disciples who are fishing see Jesus, Peter has no fear of the sea and dives straight in, swimming to meet Jesus at the shore. Then, in response to Peter's threefold, painful affirmation of his love for Jesus, Jesus instructs him to 'feed my sheep'.[8] Was this in part a reference to the disciples' failure to respond to the needs of the multitude? As we have already seen, the image of the Lord as shepherd was not lost either to the disciples or the crowd gathered at the Sea of Galilee.

Perhaps the disciples were also reminded of the fleeing and disobedient Jonah, and of the fate that awaited him. Thrown overboard by his crewmates in an effort to placate the storm caused by Yahweh because of Jonah's failure to do his will, Jonah's punishment was to be swallowed up by a sea monster.[9]

The disciples clearly feared for their very lives. We can imagine their thoughts: 'Why have we done such a foolish thing? We should have waited with the crowds for Jesus to return. I don't want to die, to be swallowed up by this dark and terrible water. I'll never see my beloved family again.' Finally, perhaps, in the midst of their despair and seeing Jesus walking towards them, they cry out against the turmoil of the storm, 'Help me, O Lord! Help me, O Lord!'

It was at this point, John tells us, that Jesus spoke just five words to the disciples. They were not words of recrimination, nor were they spoken in anger. Jesus simply says, 'It's me. Don't be afraid.'[10] We can imagine the

[7] John 21.
[8] John 21:17.
[9] Jonah 2:1.
[10] John 6:20.

calmness, stillness and purity of these words, spoken softly against the brutality and noise of the storm and the sea, and yet heard nonetheless directly in the turmoil, fear and confusion of the hearts of the disciples. 'It's me. Don't be afraid.'

Upon hearing his words, the disciples were ready to bring Jesus onto the boat, but just as they were about to do this, John tells us that they realised they had reached their destination; they had reached their journey's end. It is as if the words of Jesus pulled them not only out of their state of fear, but out of the very situation which caused that fear. The words, and the disciples' encounter with Jesus, are truly transformational.

We could, of course, leave the sign there. However, to do so would leave us in danger of missing a further and deeper richness and truth. Not for the first time in John's narrative, we must search further.

The timing of the sign and the proximity of events

In order to make true sense of the sign, we must first look at its chronological position in the Gospel. As we have seen, the fifth sign occurs immediately after the feeding of the multitude, indeed on the evening of that same day. It also immediately precedes Jesus' 'bread of life' discourse, which takes place at Capernaum on the morning of the next day. The fact that these three great events of John's narrative occur within the space of less than twenty-four hours cannot be mere coincidence.

In the Gospel of John it is the timing of events as much as the events themselves that is critical to their under- standing. Indeed, it is in the very juxtaposition of the fifth sign with both the fourth sign and the 'bread of life' discourse that we learn its true meaning. It is a meaning rooted in the personhood of Jesus and in our intimate and sacramental encounter with him today. We must therefore look again at the preceding event of the feeding of the multitude and at the succeeding event of the discourse at Capernaum. We shall then discover that the fifth sign reaches out to us now more than ever in our particular moment of history.

As we have seen, the feeding of the multitude is recorded in all three of the Synoptic Gospels, as well as in the Gospel of the beloved disciple. In the Gospel of John the narrative of the sign takes place directly after Jesus' encounter with the sick man at Bethesda and with the Jewish authorities. However, there is a natural gap in time between the two signs as the latter takes place just before the Passover,[11] whereas the healing of the sick man at Bethesda takes place at another unnamed feast.

Nevertheless, John is very specific about the timing of the fourth and fifth signs, and of the subsequent 'bread of life' discourse at Capernaum, placing all three events just before the feast of the Passover: 'The time of the Jewish Passover was near.'[12] This is no mere coincidence or error. The occurrence of the fourth and fifth signs immediately prior to the Passover celebrations is deliberate. In John's chronology, three great events of Jesus' life – the feeding of the multitude, Jesus walking on the water and the 'bread of life' discourse at Capernaum – occur not only within the space of less than a day, but also very close to the great feast of Passover.

---

[11] Some have even argued that the chronology of John's Gospel has become confused and that the events of Bethesda should take place after the feeding of the multitude.

[12] John 6:4.

For the multitude following Jesus, both on the hillside at Galilee and on the following day at Capernaum, the dramatic events of Passover would have been uppermost in their minds as they prepared to celebrate and relive the feast. As they sat at the feet of Jesus on the hillside, the impending Passover would have brought forward thoughts of liberation – a liberation brought about by sacrifice and because of God's covenant with his chosen people. They would also have been reminded, through the impending feast and the actual event of the feeding of the multitude, of the life-giving abundance of God. These themes – liberation, sacrifice and covenant, and God's life-giving abundance – were all rooted in and integral to the Passover celebrations. They defined not only the history of the Jewish people, but also their very identity and relationship with God.

All these themes are explored in Jesus' discourse at the synagogue in Capernaum. John narrates that the very next day after the fifth sign and the feeding of the multitude, the crowd followed Jesus across the Sea of Galilee to Capernaum, where they found him at the synagogue. There Jesus rebuked the crowd for following him,[13] not because they had seen the signs, but because they had had all the bread they could eat the day before and, in all probability, were seeking more.

It is here that Jesus makes his great discourse on the bread of life. He makes three key assertions. First, that he, Jesus, is the bread of life.[14] Second, that his bread represents a new covenant with God, one which has as its defining characteristic a hitherto unexperienced personal

---

[13] John 6:26.
[14] John 6:35.

and divine intimacy with God.[15] And third, that this life-giving and abundant divine intimacy is a promise for all humanity.[16]

As we shall see, there is a direct link between the themes of Passover and Jesus' assertions at Capernaum, and this synergy brings new meaning to the encounter of the disciples with Jesus on the Sea of Galilee. It is as if in the feeding of the multitude we are reminded of the great themes of Passover events, in the 'bread of life' discourse these events are given new meaning and explanation, and finally, in the encounter of the disciples with Jesus on the Sea of Galilee, we witness their fulfilment in action.

Without examining these themes in detail, therefore, we cannot truly make sense of the wonder and promise of the fifth sign – a wonder and promise made for each of us today. Thus, in the experience of liberation we hear the words of Jesus, 'I am the bread of life';[17] in the experience of sacrifice and covenant we witness Jesus as the sign of the new covenant and the promised intimacy with God; and finally, in the experience of the life-giving abundance of the Lord we hear the words of Jesus, 'my flesh [is] for the life of the world'.[18] Throughout everything, in the midst of the roaring wind and storm, in the disciples' encounter with the supranatural and sacramental Jesus, we hear his gentle words, 'It's me. Don't be afraid.'[19]

---

[15] John 6:56.
[16] John 6:58.
[17] John 6:35.
[18] John 6:51.
[19] John 6:20.

Liberation: 'I am the bread of life'

For the Jewish people, the Passover commemorated the flight of the enslaved Israelites from imprisonment and tyranny in Egypt. This escape reached its dramatic climax upon the command of Yahweh to Moses, 'raise your staff and stretch out your hand over the sea and divide it, so that the Israelites can walk through the sea on dry ground'.[20] The Israelites fled over the dry ground, while the Egyptians were left to drown in the returning waters. In remembering these events, the song of victory in honour of Yahweh would have been recalled:

> I shall sing to Yahweh,
> for he has covered himself in glory,
> horse and rider
> he has thrown into the sea...
> Pharaoh's chariots and army
> he has hurled into the sea
> the pick of his officers
> have been drowned in the Sea of Reeds.[21]

In this moment Yahweh's powerful, liberating nature is revealed. Yahweh intervenes in the history of his chosen people, a history that he has created, to liberate them. 'Sing to Yahweh, for he has covered himself in glory, horse and rider he has thrown into the sea.'[22]

How, then, is this connected to Jesus' assertions at Capernaum? At Capernaum, perhaps the most startling of Jesus' claims is his claim to be the bread of life. Within the discourse Jesus makes this claim three times, asserting 'I

[20] Exodus 14:16.
[21] Exodus 15:1, 4.
[22] Exodus 15:21.

am the bread of life'[23] twice and 'I am the living bread'[24] once. However, what is most astonishing about the claim is the language which Jesus uses. We witness here the first of the seven great 'I am' sayings to be found in the Gospel of John.[25] In using the phrase 'I am', Jesus equates himself with the very name of God that was revealed to Moses when Yahweh first appeared to him in the burning bush. There, Moses was called out to commence his mission of liberating the Israelites from Egyptian slavery:

> Moses then said to God, 'Look, if I go to the Israelites and say to them, "The God of your ancestors has sent me to you," and they say to me, "What is his name?" what am I to tell them?' God said to Moses, 'I am he who is.' And he said, 'This is what you are to say to the Israelites, "I am has sent me to you."'[26]

The holy, personal and intimate name of God is, therefore, revealed to Moses in the context of mission as Moses is called by God to serve him. Of equal importance is the fact that it is revealed to Moses and to the people of Israel in the context of promised liberation: Moses is called to bring about liberation for the people of Israel.

By using the phrase 'I am', Jesus thus makes a claim which is far greater than saying that he has been merely sent by God.[27] Rather, he asserts that he is equal to the great liberating God of the Jewish people. This revelation,

---

[23] John 6:35, 41.

[24] John 6:51.

[25] The seven 'I am' sayings contained in John are (1) 'I am the bread' (John 6:35); (2) 'I am the light' (John 8:12); (3) 'I am the gate of the sheepfold' (John 10:7); (4) 'I am the good shepherd' (John 10:11); (5) 'I am the resurrection' (John 11:25); (6) 'I am the way, I am truth and life' (John 14:6); (7) 'I am the true vine' (John 15:1).

[26] Exodus 3:13–14.

[27] Jesus has already said that the true bread of God is given to all by his Father (John 6:32–33).

like the revelation to Moses, is firmly based in the context of mission and liberation.

On hearing the words of Jesus during their encounter at the Sea of Galilee, the disciples, too, are invited to be set free, to be liberated from the slavery and tyranny of the sum of all their fears. Jesus says, 'It's me. Don't be afraid,' and at once their fears are dispelled and they are brought in peace to their journey's end. Through Jesus' gentle words they are set free; they are liberated from their fears. Fears of abandonment, fears of inadequacy, fears of failing to live up to the expectations of Jesus, fears of the violent world in which they find themselves, and fears of death are all in an instant dispelled. In the same way that the Israelites escaped through the waters of the Sea of Reeds unscathed, so the disciples arrive through the waters of the Sea of Galilee safely and at peace.

It is the same for each of us. Through the waters of our baptism we are liberated from the sum of all our fears. Through our baptism we are set free from death and are promised new life. We are invited to walk through the parted waters of fear to reach our journey's end, our own Promised Land. Yet it is easy for us to forget this fundamental and sacramental truth. We labour under the tyranny of our own fears. It is rare for us to encounter someone who truly understands what it means to live in the glorious freedom of the daughters and sons of God. Many of us, as cradle Christians, cannot recall the events of our own baptism, but we also fail in our adult lives to remember that this was the great liberating moment of our own salvation history. This was our great Passover moment. And so we forget to live out the truth of this great sacrament of liberation. We dwell in the shadows of fear.

The greatest tragedy for many of us is that we are simply

not aware of the shadows of fear in which we reside, not least because we have found a strange comfort in that place. It is, perhaps, easier to live a life confined by the fears we have allowed to be created, than to live a life of true freedom. True liberation can be a frightening thing. Many of our decisions, thoughts and actions are governed at a subconscious level by a culture of fear. In the often violent world in which we live, we are surrounded every day by visions and messages of fear. Yet Jesus, whom we encounter in the supranatural sacraments, is the same Jesus, the same 'I am who is'. And just as he called to the disciples through the waters of the Sea of Galilee, he now calls to each of us today through the waters of our baptism, 'It's me. Don't be afraid.'

The Church, also, is all too often in danger of forgetting that it is called in its mission to be a sign of hope and liberation for people and the world, rather than a sign of fear or, worse still, oppression. Yet this is the primary role of the Church: to witness to and be a sacramental sign for the world of the liberating and salvific power of the God of the people of Israel. Sadly, the Church often finds itself like the disciples' boat on the Sea of Galilee, surrounded by fearful and dark forces, she allows herself to be rocked and buffeted by them, rather than, like Jesus, transcending them and offering a vision of hope in place of a life of fear. And against a growing 'fear of criticism, fear of freedom, fear of truth; she becomes a Church of warnings rather than a Church which proclaims the Good News'.[28]

Yet now more than ever, in this particular moment of our history, against a backdrop of aggressive atheism and secularism and the voices of death growing in our society,

---

[28] Gerard W. Hughes, *In Search of a Way* (Darton, Longman & Todd, 1986).

Jesus calls to his Church, his bride, 'It's me. Don't be afraid.'

Sacrifice and covenant: 'my flesh is real food and my blood is real drink'

A precursor to and essential element of the liberation of the Israelites was the experience of sacrifice. Sacrifice was a sign of God's covenant with the people of Israel. The history of the Jewish people's relationship with Yahweh was marked by sacrifice. Consequently, the Passover feast was a celebration not only of liberation but also of God's renewed covenant with the people of Israel, a covenant that had at its heart the great promise to Abraham that he would be their God and they would be his people: 'I will shower blessings on you and make your descendants as numerous as the stars of heaven and the grains of sand on the seashore.'[29]

Even after Egypt had suffered the horrors visited upon her by the nine plagues,[30] Pharaoh refused to let the people of Israel go free. Therefore, as a final act to convince Pharaoh to release the Israelites, Yahweh promised to send his avenging angel to strike down the firstborn of every Egyptian. In this way Pharaoh would be convinced of the awesome power of the God of Israel and would sanction the release of the Israelites from their slavery. However, in order to protect the people of Israel from the same fate, the Lord commanded Moses to instruct each household to sacrifice a newborn lamb without blemish. They were to

[29] Genesis 22:17.
[30] The nine plagues were: water turned to blood; frogs; mosquitoes; horseflies; death of Egyptian livestock; boils; hail; locusts; darkness (Exodus 7 – 10).

eat this Passover meal of the lamb with unleavened bread, dressed and ready to leave immediately. In addition, on the mantels of their doors they were to daub the blood of the Passover lamb so that the avenging angel of the Lord would pass over their homes. In this way the firstborn sons of the Israelites would escape the terrible judgement that awaited the firstborn sons of the Egyptians.[31]

Through the sacrifice of a lamb, the people of Israel escaped the terrible justice of the Lord. And, as the rainbow marked the sign of God's covenant with Noah and his descendants, so the Passover lamb became a sign of God's renewed and personal covenant with the people of Israel. The God of Israel personally intervened on behalf of the Jewish people, and in so doing he entered into the now of their history:

> He, the mysterious and hidden God, had shown himself to be stronger than Pharaoh, in spite of all the power that Pharaoh could muster. Israel was never to forget that God had personally taken the history of his People in hand and that this history was based permanently on communion with God.[32]

For the people of Israel, the celebration of the Passover feast was more than just a remembrance of the deeds that God had worked for them. As Scott Hahn writes:

> Passover is more than a mere 'memorial' – more than just a commemoration of an historical event. For the Israelites, the Passover seder marked the renewal of their covenant with God. On that day, the covenant was extended in time.

---

[31] Exodus 11 – 12.
[32] Homily given by Pope Benedict XVI at the Mass of the Lord's Supper on Holy Thursday, 5 April 2007 at the Basilica of St John Lateran.

On that day they were renewed as God's people – his earthly family by covenant.[33]

And so as bread was broken and shared on the hillside at Galilee, the crowd, in remembering the events of Passover, would also have recollected the renewal of their covenant with God. In this context, the crowds and the disciples witnessed in the breaking of bread on the hillside a fore-telling of the sacrifice that Jesus would make of himself on the cross as his body was broken and his blood was spilt. They witnessed the foretelling of the beginning of a new covenant with God. Jesus would be the Paschal lamb sacrificed for all so that all could – and can – be invited to live in the glorious freedom of the sons and daughters of God. This was – and is – the new promise made by God for his people.

The crowd gathered on the hillside at Galilee also unknowingly witnessed the foreshadowing of a Eucharistic encounter with Christ, the sign of the new covenant, which was to find fulfilment in the final Passover meal shared by Jesus with the disciples just before his bloody and violent death on the cross. This theme is further explored by John in the crowd's encounter with Jesus the next day at the synagogue at Capernaum in the very claim, 'I am the bread of life.' However, in the discourse at Capernaum Jesus made the bold assertion not only that he was the liberating bread of life, but that this bread, and hence he, represented a new and different covenant with God. Having declared to the crowd, 'I am the bread of life,' Jesus, referring to Moses and the escaping Israelites, states that their fathers ate manna in the desert. Referring to himself, however, he says, 'This is the bread which has

[33] Scott Hahn, *Letter and Spirit* (Doubleday, 2005).

come down from heaven; it is not like the bread our ancestors ate: they are dead, but anyone who eats this bread will live for ever.'[34]

With these words, Jesus says something to the gathered crowd that is even more confrontational than his claim of equality with the God of their ancestors. In essence, Jesus tells them to throw away all their preconceived ideas of what it means to be a chosen people who are in covenant with God; to forget the rules and laws of the old covenant marked by the Passover of the lamb. For that direction brings only death. Here, instead, Jesus says quite simply that *he* is the sign of the new covenant. He is 'the bread of the new covenant'. For, just as the old covenant was marked with the sacrifice and blood of a lamb, so the new covenant is marked by the sacrifice and blood of Jesus.

Jesus does not stop there. He goes on to make the startling claim that his bread is real food: 'For my flesh is real food and my blood is real drink. Whoever eats my flesh and drinks my blood lives in me and I live in that person.'[35] This is an invitation to absolute intimacy. As Angel F. Méndez Montoya observes:

> When we eat, we are literally 'intimate' with food by physically bringing it near the body, lips and mouth. The ingested substance breaks the conventional boundaries of inside and outside ... and infiltrates the body with a variety of scents, textures, flavours and substances, until the ingested food is incorporated into the body through a complex metabolizing process that transforms – transfigures.[36]

---

[34] John 6:58.
[35] John 6:55–56.
[36] Angel F. Méndez Montoya, *The Theology of Food: Eating and the Eucharist* (Wiley Blackwell, 2009).

The listening crowd had followed Jesus, seeking to receive more free food as they had done on the hillside the day before. Yet here Jesus clearly states that his flesh and blood are not only real food and drink, but are the real food and drink which all must eat. This is not just an allegorical claim. It is a sacramental claim demonstrating the true intimacy of the relationship that Jesus offers to all. By eating this new Eucharistic Passover meal, we live in Jesus and Jesus lives in us. Thus to be in covenant with God, to be in relationship with God, we have to be in an intimate relationship with Jesus, an intimacy that reaches fulfilment in the Eucharist. By partaking in the Eucharist, our covenant with God is renewed and 'extended in time'.[37]

That the crowd's reaction is hostile is unsurprising as it is only now, after the events of the Last Supper and Jesus' death, that we can understand the Eucharistic significance of what Jesus is saying. What is important, however, is that Jesus describes the transforming power of the Eucharist. It is a sacrament of intimacy. By gathering round the table of the Lord and eating his bread and drinking his blood at our Eucharistic celebrations, we are transformed by Christ, because in this way Jesus lives in us and we live in him. We partake in the intimacy of God. It is little wonder that Pope Benedict XVI describes the Eucharist as 'an intimate mystery'.[38]

Jesus' words reveal a desire for intimacy, for living within each other. Jean Vanier, the founder of the L'Arche communities, writes:

---

[37] Hahn, *Letter and Spirit*.
[38] Homily given at the Mass and Eucharistic Procession on the Solemnity of Corpus Domini, 26 May 2005, in the Square in front of the Basilica of St John Lateran.

They reveal a friendship, that implies certain equality between people, each one open and vulnerable to the other. When we become a real friend to another, we give up a certain personal autonomy or freedom. In a way we die to ourselves and our needs centred on ourselves, our need to prove that we are right or are the best. ... We live one another in another. That is *mutual indwelling*.[39]

Against this background of a promised divine intimacy with and through Jesus, an intimacy which represents a new covenant with God, we can see the encounter of the disciples with Jesus on the Sea of Galilee in a new light. It is where we witness the true intimacy of the sacramental encounter of Jesus.

Jesus comes to the disciples in their utter vulnerability; he comes to them in the intimacy and thoughts of their fears, and in that intimacy he says, 'It's me. Don't be afraid.' This encounter is transformational, for in it Jesus brings them not only to a realisation of their fears, but also safely to their journey's end. From a place of fear, they are brought to place of safety, a place of courage and a place of conviction. Following the encounter, while the crowds react in a hostile manner to what Jesus has to say, the disciples themselves move from fear to conviction of faith through their transformational encounter with the supranatural Jesus. John narrates that following Jesus' discourse, many of his followers cannot understand the 'intolerable language'[40] he has used and leave him. When Jesus asks the disciples whether they too will leave, Peter responds on behalf of them all: 'Lord, to whom shall we go? You have

---

[39] Jean Vanier, *Drawn into the Mystery of Jesus through the Gospel of John* (Darton, Longman & Todd, 2004).
[40] John 6:60.

the message of eternal life.'[41] It is, perhaps, unlikely that they have truly understood Jesus' words, but they have certainly been transformed by their intimate encounter with him.

In the Eucharist we, too, encounter the supranatural Jesus, the Jesus who meets and accepts us on the sea of our fears and vulnerability. There is no judgement, there are no demands, only the promise of the gift of the trans-formational Jesus, dwelling in us and allowing us to dwell within him. Here, in the true intimacy of the sacrament of love, we meet our true selves and we meet the Lord. Like the disciples, we hear his gentle words, 'It's me. Don't be afraid.'

In its encounter with the world, the Church is called to be a sign in all that it does of this great sacrament of inti-macy. If it is to be true to this mission, the Church cannot deny this sacrament of intimacy to those who are in real need, who are drowning in the storms of their fears, no matter what the condition or state of their lives may be. It is called to offer to the world, in its pain and anguish, the opportunity to encounter the risen and intimate Jesus. In so doing the Church must reach out beyond the confines of the walls it has built around itself, perceiving itself to be under siege from the stormy seas of secularism. This is central to the mission of the Church – to be a sacramental sign of Jesus in the world and by this to offer the world a real and true sign of hope, a sign of the new covenant between God and man. And so we come to the last of the three themes of Passover: the life-giving abundance of the Lord.

---

[41] John 6:68.

The life-giving abundance of the Lord: 'flesh for the life of the world'

In the Passover story we see God demonstrating his life-giving abundance. The crowd, too, gathered on the grassy hillside witnessing and partaking in the great sign of being fed by Jesus, would have recalled two parts of scripture that emphasised this life-giving nature of their God. John tells us that the feeding of the multitude took place on a hillside near to the shore of the Sea of Galilee: 'There was plenty of grass there, and as many as five thousand men sat down.'[42] To the multitude, sitting on that verdant hillside in an otherwise dry and barren land, eating the bread that Jesus had broken would perhaps have brought to mind the words of the psalmist: 'Yahweh is my shepherd, I lack nothing. In grassy meadows he lets me lie.'[43]

But given the proximity of the Passover, they could also not have failed to recall the events following the escape of their forebears through the Sea of Reeds when Yahweh promised Moses to 'rain down bread for you from the heavens'.[44] Thus the Israelites were fed in the desert through the intercession of Moses, by manna sent from heaven: ' "That", Moses told them, "is the food which Yahweh has given you to eat." '[45] Through the words of the psalmist and the Lord's gift of manna in the desert, the life-giving abundance of the Lord is emphasised.

The theme of life-giving abundance reaches a climax at Capernaum. When Jesus declares, 'I am the bread of life,'[46]

---

[42] John 6:10.
[43] Psalm 23:1–2.
[44] Exodus 16:4.
[45] Exodus 16:15.
[46] John 6:35.

he is saying definitively that the abundance of God's sustenance comes through him and him alone; not because he has been sent by God, but because he is God.

Specifically, Jesus states that those who eat of the bread of life will not only have life but will live for ever. Again the claim is made by him a number of times in the discourse:

I am the living bread which has come down from heaven. Anyone who eats of this bread will live for ever; and the bread that I shall give is my flesh, for the life of the world.[47]

If you do not eat the flesh of the Son of man and drink his blood, you have no life in you.[48]

Anyone who does eat my flesh and drink my blood has eternal life.[49]

Whoever eats me will also draw life from me.[50]

The listening crowd at Capernaum would have found this difficult to understand. However, in the context of our own sacramental understanding, we see not only the intimate nature of the Eucharist but its life-giving and affirming quality.

The disciples' encounter with Jesus on the Sea of Galilee is literally life-giving. As we have seen, as the disciples are buffeted by the tempestuous storm they are, justifiably, in fear for their lives. For them death is a very real and near prospect; a death in the darkness of the sea surrounded by the terrible terror of the storm. Yet in the very heart of this horror Jesus intervenes. Through their encounter with Jesus they are, quite literally, brought from night to day,

[47] John 6:51.
[48] John 6:53.
[49] John 6:54.
[50] John 6:57.

from death to new life. They receive in that moment a fleeting experience of the resurrection as they are snatched from the jaws of death and led safely to new life.

Through our sacramental encounter with Jesus in the Eucharist we, too, are invited to encounter and experience the life-giving and life-affirming nature of the sacramental Jesus. Through the Eucharist we are liberated from death as we experience the divine indwelling of the life of God within us. But, critically, through the Eucharist Jesus calls us to allow his life-giving presence to change us. In our intimate meeting with Jesus through the Eucharist, we are called to be transformed through the resurrection of Christ within us. We are called to be signs of resurrection, signs of life to a world where there is so much death, darkness and despair.

The Church, too, is continually called to be a new sign of life for the entire world. It is called not only to preach the gospel of life, but to be God's sign of the gospel of life here in this world. This is a theme we will explore more fully when we look at the seventh and final sign, the raising of Lazarus, but for now we should understand that we, too, must allow the Eucharist to transform us and our communities into signs of resurrection and life.

For us, perhaps, this is the most important point. We must allow God to work within us his saving and transformational grace. To be transformed, we must say 'yes' to an awesome yet intimate life-giving God in the Eucharist. John tells us that upon hearing the words of Jesus, the apostles were ready to bring Jesus onto the boat. Frightened as they must have been, they were prepared to struggle against the raging storm to bring Jesus close to them. This was their 'yes' to God – a 'yes' which, given the circumstances, would almost certainly have meant risking their own lives further to bring Jesus safely onto the boat. However, Jesus takes them in a different and unexpected direction. The storm immediately ceases and they find themselves brought to the shores of Capernaum. When we say 'yes' to the transforming power and love of Christ in the Eucharist, when we are prepared to risk all to bring Jesus onto our boat, we do not know what shores he will lead us to or what he will ask of us, but we can be certain that in our encounter with him we will find life in abundance.

The intervention of God

John, therefore, places the feeding of the multitude firmly in the narrative of liberation, sacrifice and covenant, and in God's life-giving and sustaining grace and abundance.

These themes are all revisited and brought to full fruition in Jesus' discourse at Capernaum. And, in this context, the fifth sign of Jesus walking on the water takes on a new, exciting and sacramental meaning. Most importantly, however, Jesus declared to the crowd, and declares to us today, that his flesh is 'for the life of the world'. This intimate, life-giving sacrament is not just for the Jews, in fact it is not just for the churched. It is an intimate gift given for the whole of humanity. In this very real sense, in the Eucharist we are liberated from all that weighs us down and we are called, in mission, to be agents of liberation in the world. The challenge is how we take that gift out to the world. Pope Benedict preached, 'Nevertheless, from this intimacy that is a most personal gift of the Lord, the strength of the Sacrament of the Eucharist goes above and beyond the walls of our churches. In this Sacrament, the Lord is always journeying to meet the world.'[51]

Let us therefore summarise the further underlying meanings of the events which take place immediately prior and post to the fifth sign.

In the feeding of the multitude, John reminds us of the Passover, of God's life-giving and affirming abundance and of his covenant with the people of Israel. This theme is brought to a climax in the discourse at Capernaum, where Jesus' divinity is affirmed – a divinity that is placed in the context of mission and liberation, and within a Eucharistic foretelling of a God who will call us into a mutual and intimate indwelling with him through the breaking of bread. By gathering around the table of the Lord we are opening ourselves up not only to be transformed, but also to be agents of transformation in the world.

Our experience of the world, however, is one in which we may find it difficult to see Jesus' transformational power and in which we see, instead, so much suffering for which there is no rational answer. It is against this background that we now turn to the sixth sign – the healing of the blind man.

---

[51] Homily given at the Mass and Eucharistic Procession on the Solemnity of Corpus Domini, 26 May 2005, in the Square in front of the Basilica of St John Lateran. Published in *Behold the Lamb of God* (Family Publications, 2009).

6

'Lord, I believe'

The cure of the man born blind (John 9)

So we come to the sixth sign: the healing of the blind young man. This event takes place sometime after the events at Capernaum. Since then, the great feast of Shelters has occurred, when the Jewish people celebrated and remembered their forebears' forty years wandering in the desert and God's provision and care. The sixth sign also follows Jesus' meeting with the adulterous woman, where she is saved from being stoned to death under the harsh redress of the law. She is saved by Jesus' simple yet powerful words, 'Let the one among you who is guiltless be the first to throw a stone at her.'[1] It also follows Jesus' confrontation with the Pharisees as he preaches in the temple, where he not only declares himself to be the light of the world and the Son of Man, but dares to say to the Pharisees, 'You judge by human standards; I judge no one.'[2] Indeed, this confrontation becomes so hostile that John

---

[1] John 8:7.
[2] John 8:15.

tells us they picked up stones to throw at Jesus. He only escapes by hiding in the temple.

The sixth and penultimate sign, then, is placed in the exciting narrative of the Gospel of John, where Jesus begins to predict his own impending violent death in even more definitive terms than we found in the symbolism of the broken bread during the feeding of the multitude.[3]

In turning to the sixth sign we are faced with a growing momentum in the story of Christ. We are drawn into the excitement of events. We are ready for the next thrilling instalment and, as we shall see, we are not disappointed. The events of the sixth sign, and those that follow, represent a tipping point in the fate of Jesus – a tipping point at which even the Pharisees are divided and are forced to take sides. A tipping point at which we realise that the story of this man Jesus, a story which had begun in the joy of the wedding celebration at Cana, will not end well. A tipping point at which Jesus' violent death on the wood of the cross at Golgotha becomes an inevitable reality.

As such, the sixth sign talks to us today. It reveals clearly that, while following Jesus involves the joy of the virgin birth, it also necessarily involves the courage to face the pain of the crucifixion: 'For the wood of the crib is also the wood of the cross.'[4] The sixth sign highlights that, while the path of the Christian may have a joyous and enthusiastic start, it is not long before that path becomes rocky and painful. Nevertheless, as the fifth sign spoke to us of the intimate sacramental encounter we are invited to share, the sixth sign speaks to us of the equally divine and

---

[3] John 6:1-15.
[4] Canon Alan McLean.

intimate encounter we are invited to share in the Word of God, even in the fires of the furnace of opposition.

What is the catalyst for this dramatic turn of events in the Gospel of John? It is a young man blind from birth, begging for his very survival.

The blind young man

What do we know about the blind man? From the events that unfold we perhaps know more than we think. He is probably quite young, still young enough for his parents to be called by the Pharisees to speak on his behalf. We also know, from the way his parents react to the Pharisees' questioning, that there is little warmth, let alone a sense of protection, in their relationship with their son. When brought before the Pharisees, their reaction is not one of joy for a son who is healed, but rather one of all too quick and ready disassociation. 'He is old enough: let him speak for himself.'[5] Although this desire to disown him is born from fear – 'His parents spoke like this out of fear of the Jews'[6] – any loving parent would find it impossible to understand how fear could, in any circumstance, outweigh the sense of parental care and love for one's own child.

We know from the testimony of the young man's neighbours that he sits and begs. He knows nothing else. We also know that while he may live in a community (his neighbours are called to identify him), he is not truly part of that community. While he is known to his neighbours, he is not so well known that they are able to identify or to

---

[5] John 9:21.
[6] John 9:22.

MICHAEL REBEIRO

volunteer a name for him. Indeed, his is a solitary and lonely existence. He sits in a world of darkness, a world of fear, begging from the nameless and silent people who pass by. As such, he is not dissimilar to the man Jesus heals at Bethesda. He is invisible to those around him, and those around him are literally invisible to him too. Neither is he dissimilar to the many thousands of young people we witness on our streets every night, homeless and without food or shelter. He, like them, is outside the camp. However, we shall see that this young man's reaction to his encounter with Jesus is very different from that of the man at Bethesda.

As to the cause of the young man's blindness, we are not told. John narrates that he has been blind since birth. Whether he was born blind, or whether some tragedy occurred in the first hours or days of his young life during which he lost the precious gift of sight, we are not told. Yet, judging from the reaction of his parents, in our more cynical moments we can, perhaps, begin to conceive of an even darker tragedy.

In Danny Boyle's Oscar-winning film *Slumdog Millionaire*,[7] we witness one young street boy in Mumbai who is gifted with an angelic singing voice. Tragically he is intentionally blinded with a hot iron by his gangland owner as he will earn more money begging as a young blind singer than as a sighted one.

In the case of the blind young man, given his parents' fear and their lack of apparent affection for him, we cannot be blamed for suspecting them of some darker purpose, in which they are financially benefiting from the proceeds of

---

[7] *Slumdog Millionaire* (2008), directed by Danny Boyle and based on the novel *Q & A* by Vikas Swarup.

their son's begging. In their eyes, perhaps the young man has long since ceased to be their son, but is viewed only as a necessary financial asset from which they can benefit and earn a livelihood.

The reaction of the apostles

Upon seeing this young blind beggar at the side of the road, the apostles' response is based on preconceived assumptions. At the heart of their response is judgement. They do not see the blind young man for what he is, a victim. Neither do they see him as a brother, a fellow child of God. Nor do they seek to explore what lies beyond his physical appearance. Their judgement is immediate. Because he is blind, they see him first and foremost not as a *victim* of sin, but as a *product* of sin.

They ask Jesus, 'who sinned, this man or his parents, that he should have been born blind?'[8] It is as if they have simply not witnessed the preceding events in the life of Jesus. It seems that they have failed to understand the true reality of the God of the new covenant breaking bread with the multitude on the hillside; that they have failed to understand the loving and merciful action of God refusing to condemn the woman caught in adultery; that they have failed to hear the authoritative words of God spoken to the Pharisees in the temple, 'You judge by human standards; I judge no one.'[9]

Their question, however, was not untypical of the Jewish thought of their day. Suffering was seen as a

---

[8] John 9:2.
[9] John 8:15.

137

consequence of sin, a necessary and understandable part of the cycle of life, created by a God who would exact vengeance and judgement on those who did not follow his ways. Today we are perhaps similar to the disciples in their misunderstanding. Today, even in the context of a loving and caring Creator God, it is still difficult for us to rationalise the great suffering we witness in the world, or the suffering and anguish we go through when the pain of death or illness touches our own lives. Even when we try to see suffering with eyes of faith

> Pain can devour our spiritual sensibilities in the flames of disappointment, sadness, anger and despair. In our moments of suffering, seconds turn into hours, hours turn into months and months turn into years of struggle to survive the creative whims of evil that challenge our hopes in the promises of God.[10]

So how does Jesus respond to the disciples? His response is telling and yet also troubling. Jesus tells them that the young man is blind neither because he has sinned, nor because he has been marked by the sin of his parents. The young man's blindness is not a matter of apportioning blame. His condition is simply his condition, but it is a condition which God can use to demonstrate his loving grace, so that glory can be given to God.

Jesus' words, in themselves, are at the very least worrying. Worse, they may even appear to reveal the machinations of a fickle and hurtful God. We must ask, and legitimately so, 'Surely this young man was not born blind solely so that glory can be given to God?' Out of context of

---

[10] Robert G. Schroeder, *John Paul II and the Meaning of Suffering – Lessons from a Spiritual Master* (Our Sunday Visitor, 2008).

what has gone before and what will come after, this is not a God anyone would want to believe in, let alone be in an intimate relationship with. Here we can sympathise with the thoughts of St Teresa of Avila. As Gerard Hughes, describing his time training to be a Jesuit, wrote, 'I had often heard that God told St Teresa of Avila "I send suffering to those I love", and that she had replied "Then it is not surprising that you have so few friends." '[11]

Certainly a God who would arbitrarily inflict suffering *so that* his glory could be revealed is not the merciful God we would want to know, let alone devote our lives to out of love.

We can, however, rationalise that some of the suffering we witness in the world is caused by man's own inhumanity to man. Suffering brought about by evil is, perhaps, easier to understand. We can take comfort in its origins, which give us a certainty as to its cause and effect. Unfortunately, we all have a sense of the darkness of evil and we see the results of its work in our world all too often. We know that the suffering of those caught in the grinding and degrading poverty of the third world is caused by mankind's blindness to their condition, and by the greed of many of us in the developed world. We know that the suffering of those caught in the conflict of war is often brought about by the ideological fundamentalism of those in power. And we know that the suffering of the frightened and abused child is brought about by the selfishness and evil intent of the abuser.

However, suffering which just occurs, seemingly for no rational reason or cause, seems perverse; it goes against our innate sense of natural justice. In a world where we

---

[11] Gerard W. Hughes, *God, Where Are You?* (Darton, Longman & Todd, 1997).

strive to know the answer to everything, we demand a logical cause for the events that we experience or witness. Why is a child born with disabilities, or stillborn? Why does a mother, cursed with incurable cancer, die leaving a young and wounded family? Why is a young father laid low with multiple sclerosis, confined to a wheelchair for the rest of his days? There is no logical cause for these events, no reason, and therefore we are left in confusion and despair, a state that inevitably leads us to ask, 'If we believe in a truly loving God, why does that God allow the innocent to suffer?'

In the context of the God who does not judge, the God who will ultimately humble himself on a cross, this question, and the young man's blindness, perhaps take on new meaning. The blind young man's suffering, like the suffering of so many in the world today, is inextricably linked to the mystery of the pain and suffering of Jesus on the cross. His suffering is linked, like that of Jesus, to the suffering of the innocent. In attempting to understand this, we may find some answers in the story of Job.

The suffering of Job

Job was 'a sound and honest man who feared God and shunned evil'.[12] He was a man who, in the words of God himself, was alone in all the land in his virtue. Yet Job is noticed by Satan, who tells God that Job is only so God-fearing because God has blessed him with so much and rewarded all his endeavours. Satan argues that if God were

---

[12] Job 1:1.

to take away his possessions, then Job, too, would curse God to his face.

So it is that God agrees to test Job by putting everything he has in Satan's power. There then follows, while Job is at dinner, a series of events that, if they were not so tragic, would almost be farcical. A first messenger arrives to tell Job that his oxen and donkeys have been stolen and the servants looking after them have been put to the sword. Then a second messenger arrives with news that the fire of God has fallen from heaven and his sheep and shepherds have been burned to ashes. Almost immediately, a third messenger arrives with further news that his camels have been stolen by the Chaldeans and the attendant servants murdered. Finally, a servant arrives with news that Job's sons and daughters have been killed by their house falling upon them due to a freak weather accident. Job has suffered both at the hands of men and through the acts of God.

Yet, even in the face of such life-changing catastrophes, Job does not react at all in the way that Satan predicted. He falls to the ground saying:

> Naked I came from my mother's womb,
> naked I shall return again.
> Yahweh gave, Yahweh has taken back.
> Blessed be the name of Yahweh![13]

Satan, however, is not yet finished. He tells God, 'Someone will give away all he has to save his life. But stretch out your hand and lay a finger on his bone and flesh; I warrant you, he will curse you to your face.'[14] Again God puts Job

---

[13] Job 1:21.
[14] Job 2:4-5.

to the test and leaves him in Satan's power. Job is struck down with malignant ulcers all over his body.

At this point Job's wife loses patience, telling Job to curse God and die. Yet Job holds fast to God, refusing to blame him for his misfortune. The news of Job's plight spreads and three of his friends, Eliphaz, Bildad and Zophar, travel to be with Job and comfort him. Yet they are so shocked at seeing his plight that they sit in silence before him for seven days and seven nights.

It is only then that Job's patience with God finally breaks. His friends try to reason with him, justifying God's actions, but Job, who has led a blameless life, cannot understand how God could allow him to be so treated. In the dialogue that follows, we can empathise with Job in his suffering. The feelings and emotions he goes through are, perhaps, familiar to the way we feel when disaster strikes and we go through our own personal suffering.

In the midst of such unbearable suffering Job first rues the day he was born and, in so doing, questions the very plans of the Creator God to whom he has hitherto been faithful:

> Why was I not still-born,
> or why did I not perish as I left the womb?
> Why were there knees to receive me,
> breasts for me to suck?[15]

In Job's reaction we hear the voice of utter despair, a complete lack of hope in God. Job's sentiment finds resonance with many today who advocate the individual's right to assisted suicide in the face of life-threatening illness. Such groups hide or seek to legitimise their intent

---

[15] Job 3:11.

with language which either trivialises or couches in respectability that which they advocate. Thus they talk in terms of 'suicide tourism' or 'dignity in dying'. Indeed, the Swiss group set up in the 1960s to advocate assisted suicide, and which now operates clinics where such practices are legal, uses the expression 'dignitas' to describe itself.

Personally, I doubt that the motives of many involved in or advocating such activities are born out of a truly malicious or evil intent. But these motives, no matter how noble they may feel them to be, reveal in the face of suffering a fundamental despair and lack of faith in a loving Creator God – a God who, from such love, presents the precious gift of life to each of us.

Job cannot understand why he is suffering. It goes against his fundamental belief in a just and loving God, a belief which has hitherto lain at the core of his untested faith. If he has done something wrong, then he is prepared to accept God's punishment. Job laments:

> Put me right, and I shall say no more;
> show me where I have been at fault.[16]

At the heart of Job's pain is the knowledge that he has not offended God. It is not surprising, then, that such pain begins to turn to bitterness:

> He who crushes me for one hair,
> who, for no reason, wounds and wounds again,
> not even letting me regain my breath,
> with so much bitterness he fills me![17]

It is equally unsurprising that Job's bitterness and resentment is soon directed not only at God but at his fellow

---

[16] Job 6:24.
[17] Job 9:17–18.

man. He becomes jealous of the good fortune of those around him. Job cannot understand why those who have led less virtuous lives than him escape God's punishment. For Job, this adds insult to his injuries:

> And yet the tents of brigands are left in peace:
> those who provoke God dwell secure.[18]

We know that Job is not alone in his reaction. It is as if it were almost part of the human condition to feel envy. Perhaps this is because we feel, from our own sense of misguided justice, that we should all be treated equally. When others are more fortunate than us, we want a share of their fortune. When we suffer, sometimes the darker part of us wants others to suffer too. We feel aggrieved that we suffer alone. And yet this thinking leads us away from God. We put ourselves in the position of judge of our destiny and the destiny of his people. In so doing, not only do we question God's thinking and his creative salvation history for each of us, but we seek again to place ourselves on a parity with him, to be his equal. Our human judgement is placed in direct opposition to that of God. This, however, only leads us further and further from God and his loving kindness.

It is not surprising that Job, in his sufferings, begins to feel an alienation from the God he has loved for the entirety of his life. No longer is he the intimate God of Job's past. For Job, in his suffering, God is aloof and far away:

> If I go to the east, he is not there;
> or to the west, I still cannot see him.
> If I seek him in the north, he is not to be found,

---

[18] Job 12:6.

invisible as ever, if I turn to the south.[19]

In his suffering Job feels utterly abandoned by the God to whom he has been faithful. For Job, God has become cruel and capricious, a God who is now punishing him without just cause:

I cry to you, and you give me no answer;
I stand before you, but you take no notice.
You have grown cruel to me,
and your strong hand torments me unmercifully.[20]

We, too, share in Job's despair. Often, when we suffer or witness the suffering of those we love, we feel abandoned by God. When we are in great pain and distress it is often difficult to see God.

When I was a young student at the seminary, I visited a Benedictine monk who was dying. Separated from the daily rhythm and love of the community in which he had spent his life, he was now cared for in his final days by nuns in a nursing home. As I sat with him, he lay in his bed in great agony, waiting for the end to come. In the crassness of my youth I tried to console him, pointing out that at least now, released from the duties assigned to him in the monastery, he was able to spend his time in prayer. He looked at me with anger in his eyes and said, 'I cannot pray, I am in too much pain.' At the time I was shocked by the violence of his response, particularly from a priest I had admired as a man of great peace, serenity and faith. On reflection, however, the only shocking thing was my own youthful naivety and the insensitivity of my words. In our pain it sometimes feels impossible to reach out to God.

---

[19] Job 23:8–9.
[20] Job 30:20–21.

Nevertheless, although we may feel abandoned by God, it is a sure and certain truth that God has not abandoned us, that he walks with us holding and comforting us. How, then, does God respond to Job?

The mystery of suffering

God replies to Job from the 'heart of the tempest'. We might be tempted to interpret this as a sign of a mighty God shouting at Job from the centre of a mighty storm. However, in my view, perhaps the tempest from which God speaks is the storm raging within Job himself. Perhaps the words and the way in which God speaks to Job are not so much an indication of a loud, thundering and fearsome God, but rather a God who speaks quietly in Job's heart. Read in this light, the words that God speaks to Job perhaps take on a gentleness which would otherwise be too easy to overlook. This is the God of Elijah,[21] speaking to Job through the still, small voice.

God's immediate response to Job is to question the grounds on which he doubts God. 'Who are you to ask these questions, to question my will? Who are you to know better, Job – do you think you have the same knowledge as God?' There follows a beautiful passage in which God, by interrogating Job, clearly demonstrates that he alone is the master of all creation. Only he, therefore, can know the reason for Job's suffering. God asks:

Where were you when I laid the earth's foundations?
Tell me, since you are so well-informed![22]

---

[21] 1 Kings 19:12–13.
[22] Job 38:4.

Have you ever in your life given orders to the morning
or sent the dawn to its post,
to grasp the earth by its edges
and shake the wicked out of it?[23]

Have you visited the place where the snow is stored?
Have you seen the stores of hail,
which I keep for times of distress,
for days of battle and war?
From which direction does the lightning fork,
where in the world does the east wind blow itself out?
Who bores a channel for the downpour
or clears the way for the rolling thunder
so that rain may fall on lands where no one lives,
and the deserts void of human dwelling,
to meet the needs of the lonely wastes
and make grass sprout on the thirsty ground?[24]

Faced with such questions, Job can only concede that it is
not his place to question God. He retracts what he has said.
The story ends well for Job because God restores him to
his good fortune and more.

So what can we learn from the story of Job? For those
who demand a clear and logical answer to the question of
why the innocent suffer, ultimately the story of Job will
leave them unsatisfied. Job's story does not give us a clear
answer; there is no logical argument to be made. In the
final analysis the mystery of the suffering of the innocent
remains just that, a mystery, connected in some way to
God's creative plan for the entirety of his creation.

This mystery of suffering lies at the heart of the human
condition. We neither know the mind of God, nor can we

---

[23] Job 38:12–13.
[24] Job 38:22–27.

claim to know with any certainty God's plan for each of us. We can, however, be certain that we do not have a vengeful or capricious God. If it were not for his condition, the young blind man would not have encountered Christ.

It is tempting, and far too easy, to offer trite and simplistic answers to a demanding world regarding the meaning of suffering. To do so, however, would be to simplify God and to claim a knowledge which is equal with his. Further, in so doing we would be little better than Job. We cannot offer simple solutions to what is, at its very heart, a mystery of faith. As a doubt-led Church, we can only offer the 'loving kindness of the heart of our God who visits us like the dawn from on high'.[25]

It is in our suffering that we meet the Lord. We meet him on the cross, suffering in a bloody agony for us, experiencing selflessly the pain of our humanity. It is as if, because of our flawed natures and our overpowering egos, only in suffering can we begin to recognise our true place in the world, to recognise our own lack of divinity. Only at that moment can we recognise the true divinity of Christ and the true humanity of ourselves.

But there is another element to the mystery of our suffering that we should not ignore. For God can use our suffering for his own purposes and for his own good. In this context, suffering takes on a spiritual power; one that, although we cannot understand it, can be used for God's purpose:

'Through the Resurrection, he manifests the victorious power of the suffering, and he wishes to imbue with the conviction of this power the hearts of those whom he

---

[25] Luke 1:78, translation from the Divine Office Benedictus.

chose as Apostles and those whom he continually chooses and sends forth.'[26]

Through our suffering we are joined to the suffering of the innocent Christ on the cross. Through our suffering we join in the redemptive act of the suffering of Christ and, in so doing, we live out our baptismal mission:

> Faith in sharing the suffering of Christ brings with it the interior certainty that the suffering person 'completes what is lacking in Christ's afflictions'; the certainty that in the spiritual dimension of the work of the Redemption he is serving, like Christ, the salvation of his brothers and sisters.[27]

Let us now return to the story of the blind young man, for it is in his response to suffering that we can learn much for our time.

In the midst of suffering: 'I am the light of the world'

John tells us that Jesus makes a paste with his spit and some earth and then puts this paste over the eyes of the young man.[28] He tells the man to go to the pool of Siloam, which means 'one who is sent', and wash. On the young man's return, he is cured.

The mechanics of Jesus' healing of the young blind man are very different from anything that has gone before. The royal official's son is healed on the word of Jesus, as is the man at Bethesda who, on Jesus' word, picks up his mat and walks around. Here, however, the manner of the blind

---

[26] John Paul II, *Salvifici Doloris*:25.
[27] Ibid.:27.
[28] John 9:6.

man's cure seems almost cruel. First, Jesus puts spit and earth over his eyes. To spit at someone would have been an insult, but to take that spit and put it over a person's eyes would have seemed far worse.

However, there is a rich symbolism present here that we should not overlook. Jesus makes the paste from spit and earth. Spit is saliva, which is over ninety per cent water. Saliva acts as a natural disinfectant – it purifies. But, more importantly in this context, without saliva we could neither taste nor speak. In one sense, saliva is the medium through which we receive nourishment and through which our words are carried. As Jesus mixes his spit with the earth, we are reminded not only of the story of creation,[29] but also that it is from the very earth that we derive life. Without soil we would have no plant life. Without plant life not only would we have no vegetation for us to eat and for our livestock to feed upon, but we would have no air to breathe. It is not without reason that the great rainforests of the Amazon are called the lungs of the world. And for this reason, if for no other, as stewards of God's creation we should rightly be concerned about their gradual destruction.

Thus we see Jesus mixing the medium of the word with the medium of life. And the Word of God literally brings a new life to the once-blind young man, a life no longer lived in darkness but a life lived in light. Here, then, is the direct challenge for us today. Jesus calls us to be the medium of life, always receptive to the Word of God and, hence, agents of new life for a suffering world living in darkness. The Word is given that we might listen and, in listening, act.

---

[29] Genesis 1.

Christians in the Catholic tradition are perhaps, on a subconscious level, a little less open to or comfortable with the Word of God that is found in Scripture than our Protestant sisters and brothers. It was not so long ago that it would have been surprising to find a Bible in a Catholic household. As a young boy growing up in a staunchly Catholic family, I can remember being called together to pray the rosary in times of trouble, but never to read Scripture. It was not that my parents had any aversion to the Word of God, but rather that the Word was something shared only once a week at the celebration of the Eucharist. Likewise, it is not that the Church has become over-reliant on the expression of tradition, but rather that we fail to listen to the Word of God outside the celebration of that tradition. But tradition can only find its focus, its life, its true guidance and balance from the Holy Spirit if it is firmly based in the Word of God.

If we are to be agents of change and signs of hope for the world, then we must be nourished by both tradition and Scripture, by both sacrament and the Word, because it is the Word of God that gives sense to our tradition. One of the past participants in our Journey in Faith programme in Bermondsey was a taxi driver. He was born into an Irish Catholic family, but drifted away from the Church in his youth. It was only many years later, when a passenger left him a Bible which he started to read in between fares, that he began to feel drawn back to the traditions of the Church. Both he and his wife are now active members of the church community and, having gone through the process of evangelisation themselves, are now part of the evangelisation team leading others on the journey of faith in search of the Lord. It was the Word of God which led

151

them both to a new life, one based jointly on tradition and on the Word of God.

Jesus tells the blind young man to go the pool at Siloam to wash. Compared to the simple command to the sick man at Bethesda, where we are told that Jesus said, 'Get up, pick up your sleeping-mat and walk around,'[30] reading these words we can sometimes forget the enormity of the task which Jesus asks the young man to undertake. Jesus tells him to find his own way to the pool at Siloam and to wash. However, at this point he is still blind. We can imagine the young man trapped in a world of darkness, stumbling along a rocky path, perhaps falling as he trips over unforeseen obstacles in his path, cutting or bruising his face or hands as he reaches out in that darkness, trying desperately to steady himself and not to fall. Slowly, and desperately, he tries to edge ever closer to the pool at Siloam. It is only then, after washing his eyes in the pool, that he is healed. The theatrics of this sign seem to be at the expense of the already suffering young man, to add further insult to his injury. But here, once again, we find that there is more to the narrative of John.

Having received the Word of God, the young man is sent on his own journey of faith. At this stage the Word of God is already beginning to have a transformative effect upon him, but one of which he can make little or no sense. He starts his blind journey searching for the pool so he can wash himself. He acts upon the Word, but he does not know where this will lead him. Jesus has told him to wash himself in the pool, but has expressly not said that by doing so he will be healed. Again, this is very different from the healing of the man at Bethesda, where John tells us that

---

[30] John 5:8.

when Jesus speaks the words, 'Get up, pick up your sleeping-mat and walk around',[31] the man is instantaneously healed. The actions of the young man at Siloam are, therefore, both literally and symbolically a journey of blind faith. Moreover, even though there has been no express promise made by Jesus that his hopes will be fulfilled, touched by the Word of God the young man moves forward in hope and expectation.

The blind young man also starts his journey from a position of exclusion. His blindness has resulted in him living as a beggar and as an outcast from society. To many he has become faceless, just like the sick man at Bethesda. Even some of his neighbours who are later brought before the Jewish authorities are not able to identify him with certainty. As we shall see, what is even more startling is that while the young man starts his faith journey from outside the community, he ends it in exactly the same place – ejected by the Jewish community because of his own growing realisation of the divinity of Jesus. And when Jesus finds him at the end of the story, he is once again alone. On this occasion, however, his life has been forever transformed by his encounter with Jesus.

There are three important points from which we can learn here. First, the man's journey to physical and spiritual enlightenment is not an easy one. Touched by the Word of God, the man embarks upon a painful and difficult journey. Coming to believe in Jesus may not always be a comfortable experience. Indeed, if our faith is cosy and relaxed, then perhaps something is wrong. True faith in Jesus, a true encounter with the Word of God, will always lead us along a challenging and difficult path, on an unknown

---

[31] Ibid.

journey. A deacon I once knew always ended his blessing with the words, 'May the Spirit of God disturb you today.' And this is the challenge to the Church today, where the Word of God encounters living tradition. Tradition, in its practice, is always challenged by the Spirit to change and evolve, to find new ways of expressing the same and eternal truth which lies at the heart of our faith:

> We must never forget that all authentic and living Christian spirituality is based on the Word of God proclaimed, accepted, celebrated and meditated upon in the Church. This deepening relationship with the divine word will take place with even greater enthusiasm if we are conscious that, in Scripture and the Church's living tradition, we stand before God's definitive word on the cosmos and on history.[32]

Second, as we travel in hope and expectation on our own journey in faith, we will, like the blind young man, often stumble and fall. We will often make the wrong choices and take the wrong paths. We will stumble on the rocks in our path as we struggle to see and find a way through the darkness, even when we have been touched by the Word of God. This is both part of the human condition and part of the condition of the development of our faith. We must learn to be accepting and forgiving of our own failures and frailties because it is only in so doing that we can begin to be accepting and forgiving of the spiritual failures of our brothers and sisters. If we could only see ourselves through the eyes of our eternally and unconditionally loving God, how different we would be!

Finally we, as the Church, must always position ourselves in a place which is, in some way, outside the

---

[32] Benedict XVI, *Verbum Domini: Post-Synodal Apostolic Exhortation on the Word of God* (2010).

comfort of the communal tent, outside the camp. Like the young man, we will often start and end our journey of faith outside the comfort of civil society. We are a community of believers who, while coming from and living within the secular community, must not allow ourselves to be ruled by that community. This means that we must always challenge ourselves, the Church and, indeed, civil society as a whole to live according to the gospel and Kingdom values with which God has entrusted us. Positioning the Church as such means, too, that it will necessarily come into conflict with society as it becomes the voice in the wilderness preparing a way for the Lord.

'Do you believe in the Son of Man?'

'So he went off and washed and came back able to see.'[33] By washing himself in the pool at Siloam, the young man regains his sight. Again, the language of John's narrative is rich in symbolism. As we have seen, the young blind man has had to find the pool. In response to being touched by the Word of God, an action takes place, an initial indication that he is willing to go on a journey which is the precursor to his sight being restored. Unlike the man who is healed at Bethesda, here the young blind man must do something. And from that initial action he is led on a journey which will change his life for ever.

By washing himself in the waters at Siloam, the young man is cleansed; his sight is restored and with his new sight he is given the transformational gift of a new life. However, at this stage he has no inkling of what the simple

---

[33] John 9:7.

action of washing himself will lead to. He has no idea that in a matter of days he will find himself arguing with the Pharisees and being ejected by them. He has no idea that he will have a further encounter with Jesus and, through a discovery of faith, come to acknowledge him as the Son of Man.

In the same way, through our own baptism we are made clean and our new lives in faith begin. As we saw in the fifth sign, most of us who are baptised at birth are far too young to make sense of the event, let alone understand the implications of the baptismal promises which are made on our behalf by our godparents. My infant son at his baptism, in an effort to avoid the baptismal waters being poured over his head, made a lunge for the Paschal candle, nearly knocking it over, while screaming at the top of his voice, 'No church! No church!' This was not the reaction of a child possessed, but rather that of a little boy scared at being the centre of attention, who was going through a phase of hating water on his face. Yet now, only a few years later, as his relationship with Jesus has grown, his bedtime routine is not truly complete without a nightly conversation with his friend Jesus.

Through and following baptism, as we physically mature, so we grow and mature in faith and are nourished by the Word of God and by the sacraments. Our faith, however, is never complete; we continue to grow. So it is with the young man. But, as with the young man, there comes a point at which we must be prepared to move from the infancy of faith to a positive acknowledgement of who Jesus is for each of us – not as the God of our childhood, not as the God of our parents and not as the God of the Church, but as our personal Lord and Saviour. It is at this point that we take on the faith of our parents for ourselves; we embrace it and try to live it. But we must acknowledge and embrace it as our own, rather than simply wear it like an old overcoat to which we have become accustomed. We may wear it grudgingly, but without really understanding why we are reluctant to discard it. It is at this point that the practice of our faith must move from habit to a positive decision.

I remember for me that point came when I reached sixteen. It was then, in the face of cynicism from my peers, that I had to decide whether or not I wanted to continue in the practice of the faith of my parents or to make that faith my own, something to be treasured and, most importantly, something to be lived. For all of us who are parents the temptation may be, as our children grow into their teens, to insist that they wear our old overcoats of faith. However, we must give our children the space and the freedom to find the faith that they can embrace and hold as their own. A parent's role is not to 'pass on the faith', but rather to witness to the truth of his or her own faith in their life, to share that faith and, most importantly, simply to provide a safe spiritual space for their children to grow.

The young man, on being healed by Jesus, does not immediately believe that Jesus is his Lord and Saviour. It is not through his initial encounter with Jesus that he finds an instant, ready-made faith. Rather, it is in the testing in the fire of a hostile environment that his small seed of faith begins to grow. The young man goes through a threefold development of his faith, and in each stage it is because his faith is tested under the intense scrutiny of others that it is able to grow.

After being healed, he encounters his neighbours and the people who knew him when he was a blind beggar. Their reaction is mixed. Some believe him to be the man they know. Others, even though the evidence is right there, find it easier to believe that the healed young man before them is someone else, rather than accept that Jesus has cured him. When questioned as to how he was healed, he declares that it was the *man* called Jesus who made a paste, daubed his eyes with it and then told him to wash. Thus, under the scrutiny of those with whom he is familiar, and those who are familiar with him, he declares Jesus to be a man.[34] If he were to stay here, then, in the comfort of familiarity, even under challenge his faith would not grow.

His neighbours, however, then take him to the Pharisees. We must remember that at this stage Jesus had already had numerous life-threatening encounters with the Pharisees, and John tells us that they had already agreed that anyone who acknowledged Jesus as the Anointed One, the Christ, would be banned from the synagogue.[35]

The Pharisees are immediately thrown into disarray by the appearance of the young man. Some argue that, as Jesus performed the miracle on the Sabbath, he cannot be from God. Others argue that unless he was from God he could not have performed such an act, whether the act occurred on the Sabbath or not. For the young man this must have been a terribly frightening experience. To be brought before the Pharisees in the temple would have been daunting enough for anyone. But he had spent his life excluded from the community, and coupled with the fact that he would have known he was the catalyst of the dispute among the Pharisees, this experience must have been truly petrifying. Yet, despite this, when they ask the young man who he thinks Jesus is, he does not revert to the

[34] John 9:11.
[35] John 9:22.

answer he gave amongst the familiarity of his neighbours. Instead, he is emboldened by the experience and replies, 'He is a prophet.'[36]

The Jews next bring the young man's parents before them. His parents admit that he is their son and that he has been blind from birth, but they deny any knowledge of how he came to be healed. As we have already discussed, John tells us that they speak in this way because they are afraid. Strangely, as we have seen, there is no rejoicing; no overt moment of happiness comes with the knowledge that their son has been healed. There is no real closeness displayed here, no tenderness. If it had not been for the presence of their neighbours, perhaps they would have tried to deny all knowledge of their son. Yet John strongly implies that they know Jesus has cured him and, rather than testify on their son's behalf, they abandon him to the Pharisees: 'He is old enough: let him speak for himself.'[37] Because they cannot bear the thought of being outside the camp, they place fear of the Pharisees and a love of synagogue above love of their son.

This is in stark contrast to the young man himself, who now comes to argue with the Pharisees. Here is a man who is not educated, who has been blind for the entirety of his life, who has dwelt in an outer and inner world of darkness and yet, once touched by the Word of God, he finds a voice of courage and is emboldened to speak the truth as he has experienced it.

Indeed, the Pharisees demand that he tells the truth – provided it is the truth as they have come to see it: 'Give glory to God! We are satisfied that this man is a sinner.'[38]

---

[36] John 9:17.
[37] John 9:21.
[38] John 9:24.

They are bound by the shackles of their orthodox fundamentalism in which there is no room for doubt. When the
young man responds by saying he does not know whether
Jesus is a sinner or not, all he knows is that Jesus healed
him, the Jews demand to know how Jesus has healed him.
Whereas the young man can only speak of the truth from
his experience of Jesus, the Jews root their arguments
firmly in the law and in logic: if he has healed on the
Sabbath, he cannot be of God. The argument ends with the
young man declaring that if Jesus were not of God, he
would not have been able to do anything. Even in the heat
of the battle, in the heat of the argument, surrounded by
the shouting and angry crowd and in the unfamiliarity of
the synagogue, the young man's faith is not weakened. On
the contrary, it is strengthened and enlightened. It is here,
in this moment, that the young man begins to glimpse
more – more, perhaps, than even the disciples have seen –
of the reality of who Jesus is. He begins to see Jesus no
longer as man or as prophet, but as being of God.

The Pharisees at this point are so angry that they begin
to hurl abuse at the young man and eject him from the
synagogue with these words, 'Are you trying to teach us,
and you a sinner through and through ever since you were
born!'[39] The young man with his new-found sight sadly
witnesses the ugliness of humanity, for with these words
the Pharisees firmly close their eyes to the new revelation
of Christ. They entrench themselves in and only identify
with the rule-based old law. They reject the new covenant.
The Pharisees do not allow their tradition to be inspired by
the Word of God. Their tradition is not alive. It is dead.
With that one phrase, uttered unanimously, the battle lines

---

[39] John 9:34.

are firmly drawn. How sad it is that we sometimes hear that same battle cry today in our Church; see that same resistance to change, that same resistance to the Word of God, inspired and motivated by the Holy Spirit, moving through and in the Church. The Spirit does not call the Church to reinvent the truth, but does call the Church constantly to evolve in praxis the reality of that truth.

It is at this point that the young man's faith faces its final test. It is now that he must make his final commitment. John tells us that on hearing he has been ejected from the synagogue, Jesus seeks the young man out. Jesus then asks him whether he believes in the Son of Man. The young man replies, 'Tell me who he is so that I may believe in him.'[40] When Jesus tells him that he is the Son of Man, the young man replies, 'Lord, I believe,'[41] and worships him. It is at this point that the beginning of his faith journey is complete.

We do not know what happened to the young man after that. One would like to think that he left his family and became a follower of Jesus, perhaps a leader of the early Church. Certainly the eloquence and courage of his speech in the synagogue compares well with the speeches of Peter and Paul witnessing to the risen Christ. However, we will, in truth, never know with any certainty what happened to the young man. We can, though, learn much from his story. We can begin to touch upon the mystery of suffering and the suffering of innocence. We too can learn from both his reaction to suffering and his journey to discover faith. Although the seed of his faith is planted through his encounter with the Word of God, the seed

---

[40] John 9:36.
[41] John 9:38.

161

does not grow in the comfort of familiarity but in the furnace of challenge and opposition. His is a journey which the Lord calls us and the Church to travel every day of our lives. We, too, must live and experience the heat and fire of the furnace of opposition if our faith is truly to grow.

And so we near the end of our journey and move on to the seventh and final sign, the raising of Lazarus. It is in this sign that we discover the true extent of the furnace of opposition that we, as the followers of Christ, face in the world today.

7

'Lazarus, come out!'

The resurrection of Lazarus (John 11:1–43)

The raising of Lazarus is the climax of an unfolding drama. Here John brings us to the closing part of Jesus' public ministry of the signs, a ministry that finds its conclusion in a time of conflict and confrontation. To place it in context, the seventh sign takes place immediately before Jesus' triumphant entry into Jerusalem; before the intimate Passover feast shared with the disciples; before the trial and subsequent bloody death of Jesus at Golgotha.

Prior to the occurrence of the seventh sign, and following a confrontation with the Jewish authorities in the temple during the feast of Dedication, John tells us that Jesus has to leave in order to escape being stoned by the crowds for claiming to be God.[1] This is a far cry from the events of the fifth sign, immediately following the feeding of the multitude, when Jesus also had to leave in secret to avoid the crowd. Then, however, it was not because the

---

[1] John 10:33, 'We are stoning you, not for doing a good work, but for blasphemy; though you are only a man, you claim to be God.'

crowd wanted to kill him, but rather because they wanted to crown him king. Indeed, it is the completion of the seventh sign that leads to the express decision of the Jewish authorities to crucify Jesus.[2] Caiaphas argues that Jesus should be put to death because it is better for one man to die for the people.[3]

After the raising of Lazarus, Jesus becomes a wanted man and the chief priests and the Pharisees give orders that anyone who knows of his whereabouts must inform them so that he can be arrested.[4] We have come a long way on our journey from the joy and love of community witnessed at Cana in the first sign. The seventh sign is surrounded by an increasing sense of darkness and impending death. Perhaps, then, it is not surprising that Jesus should elect to perform a final sign which is rooted in death itself.

It is in this darkness of death that Jesus reveals to us the nature of the truly transformational power of a loving and compassionate God. This is the culmination of his pastoral mission as revealed in the signs: to show that even death has no power over him, and no power, hence, over his followers. Jesus shows us once again that even in the face of death, we are called to be signs of new life and resurrection. In a world where so much of humanity dwells in a culture or under the shadow of death, and in a world which in so many ways is violently opposed to the gospel of life, the importance of this concluding sign cannot be underestimated.

Let us remind ourselves of the story of the seventh sign. Jesus, now on the far side of the Jordan, receives word that his friend Lazarus has been taken ill. However, despite the

[2] John 11:45–53.
[3] John 11:50.
[4] John 11:57.

urging of the disciples, Jesus does not rush to his side. Rather, he waits a further two days before setting off for Bethany, the home of Lazarus and his two sisters, Martha and Mary. When Jesus does finally elect to go to Bethany, the same disciples urge caution because of its proximity to Jerusalem (it is only some two miles away) and the ensuing danger to Jesus' life. Yet Jesus continues on his journey and on his way to the house of Lazarus is met by Martha. She has heard that Jesus is coming and has rushed out to meet him. She tells Jesus that Lazarus has already died and has been in the tomb for four days. Yet she says to Jesus, 'Lord, if you had been here, my brother would not have died, but even now I know that God will grant whatever you ask of him.'[5] Although Jesus promises that Lazarus will rise again, he makes no promise that this will be now rather than in the afterlife. Nevertheless, Martha affirms her belief in Jesus as 'the Christ, the Son of God, the one who was to come into this world'.[6]

Martha then returns to Mary in Bethany. Mary is waiting at their home with the gathered mourners who have come to share in their sorrow, and Martha tells her that Jesus is on his way. On hearing this news Mary and the mourners immediately go to meet Jesus and there, on the road, distraught with grief, Mary throws herself at Jesus' feet, overcome by heartache and anger. In the narrative she seems almost to rebuke him: 'Lord, if you had been here, my brother would not have died.'[7] While Mary uses almost identical words to Martha, this time there is no affirmation or expression of faith in Jesus. Mary's and the mourners' reactions greatly distress Jesus, in fact to the point of tears.

---

[5] John 11:21.
[6] John 11:27.
[7] John 11:32.

Nevertheless, he is not deterred. On reaching the tomb of Lazarus, notwithstanding the protests of Martha, who says that after four days the smell of Lazarus's body will be overwhelming, Jesus commands that the covering stone of the tomb be removed. Once this is done, he calls to Lazarus to come out of the tomb. And, at the word of Jesus, still bound by the burial robes in which he has been laid, Lazarus comes out. Jesus then commands that Lazarus be unbound, releasing him from the captivity of death.

What can we learn from this sign? As we have seen, the events at Bethany represent the conclusion of an unfolding drama in the life of Christ. It is the final sign. And, as such, there is much that we can learn, not only from each of the central characters in this final act, but also from the very nature of the sign itself, the act of resurrection. And it is here that we must begin.

'Lazarus, come out!'[8]

On reflection, it may appear that the six signs Jesus has completed up to this point in John's narrative are as nothing when compared to the events that take place at Bethany. They all seem to fade in significance when compared to the resurrection of Lazarus from the dead.

Each of the previous signs was a symbol of God's intervention in the 'now' of the lives of the people Jesus encountered in Judea. In undertaking these signs, Jesus used the interventions to witness to a truth of the nature of God, his Father – that God walks with us individually in the everyday moments of our lives; that God is not only

[8] John 11:43.

concerned with the fate of humanity throughout the sweep of history, but intimately concerned with our individual fates as his sons and daughters. He accompanies us on our own journeys of faith, life and love, never leaving our side, no matter how we may react to his presence. In so doing, Jesus has also shown us the nature of the Church's threefold royal, prophetic and priestly mission: to reach out to, and walk with, all people in the intimacy of sacramental love and the Word of God.

At Cana, Jesus intervenes in the 'now' of the celebration of true communion and community, but also in the 'now' of the celebration of intimate love in the communion between man, woman and God. In the healing signs at Cana, Bethesda and Siloam, Jesus shows the power of God's love in the midst of our individual doubt, alienation and suffering. And in the feeding of the multitude and in the act of Jesus walking on the water, we discover the nature of mission and the intimacy of Christ in our lives through sacrament and Word.

The seventh sign, however, is a sign of God's intervention not into the life of men and women, but into their very death. As such, it represents the culmination of the signs. It is the foreshadowing of Christ's own resurrection and in it we witness the triumph of Jesus over death. In this certainty of resurrection we find the promise of new life for each of us, the promise which must lie at the very heart of our faith. In the seventh sign we witness that Jesus walks with us through both life and death. That truth is the good news of the gospel and exists for all humanity. As such, the seventh sign takes centre stage in the salvific mission of the Church throughout all time.

In television medical dramas such as *Casualty* or *ER,* we witness people being brought back from the brink of death by the wonders of modern science and the skills of medical professionals. As science progresses, we may begin to have faith that knowledge will prolong our lives and delay death. However, science has its boundaries and it cannot – and should not – reach out beyond the realms of God's natural order. In the case of Lazarus, science could not have been relied upon.

We do not know the cause of Lazarus's death. Yet we do know that he had been in the tomb, dead, for four days. His raising, even by today's standards, would have been viewed as impossible. To the witnesses at Bethany it was nothing short of divinely miraculous. Even more so as Jewish custom at the time stated that the soul hovered with the corpse for three days – until the body burst open – then left the body. In light of this, as Craig A. Evans argues, 'Jesus' ability to raise Lazarus, dead for four days, would have been viewed as astounding'.[9]

Let us think for a moment what it must have been like in that tomb with Lazarus. On his death, Lazarus's body would have been washed, then wrapped in burial garb and scented with oils. After four days, however, his body would have been in a state of decomposition. It would have passed through rigor mortis and begun a state of putrefaction, releasing gases produced by bacteria working on and in the body. Given the hot and humid climate in Judea, this process may even have been accelerated. It is certain that after four days the tomb, a cave in which Lazarus's body had been laid, would have begun to smell horribly of the stench of death. Indeed, Martha warns Jesus not to remove the covering stone from the cave in which

---

[9] For a much fuller examination of Jewish burial customs, see Craig A. Evans, *Jesus and the Ossuaries: What Burial Practices Reveal about the Beginning of Christianity* (Baylor University Press, 2003).

Lazarus has been buried: 'Lord, by now he will smell; this is the fourth day since he died.'[10] Moreover, the Jewish people would have viewed Lazarus's body as ritually unclean. It could not be touched under any circumstances.

Not only would the stench of Lazarus's putrefying body have been present in the tomb, but the tomb itself would have been in complete darkness. No light would have penetrated past the covering stone into the cave where Lazarus lay bound. This place, then, was indeed the embodiment of death itself from which there could be no escape. And, as we think of that dark tomb, we begin to feel uncomfortable. We are reminded of our own mortality and our natural inclination is to recoil, to escape. Death, even today, remains the final taboo. We feel uneasy discussing it openly. When we are directly touched by death, through the loss of a neighbour or loved one, our natural tendency is to focus on the grief of loss rather than on the details of the death itself. The tomb is not a place in which we wish to linger, let alone dwell at a conscious level. We naturally run from death.

Yet, on another level, we have become immune, and almost a ready companion, to death. We see and hear of death on our news screens every day, whether through war, murder, poverty or natural disaster. Our young people even rejoice in death and destruction through films and video and computer games. We are in danger of letting death regain its dominion over ourselves and society. At a personal and subconscious level we have become comfortable dwelling in the tomb.

If we take a moment to reflect, although we will see much of goodness, life and light in the way we live our

---

[10] John 11:39.

lives, in moments of true honesty we will also see parts, in our ingrained behaviour perhaps, where we have become strangely more comfortable in the stink and darkness of the tomb. In some cases we have become so comfortable dwelling in this dark space that we are afraid to come out into the glorious light and life-giving fresh air of God. Often it is easier to hold on to our bitterness, our anger, our hatred of others than to swallow our pride and admit our own failings. It is easier to hold on to broken and difficult relationships than to reach out to each other for healing in love. And it is easier to blame ourselves, to hold on to our own guilt, than to accept the forgiveness of a loving and tender God. But these are all signs of death, not signs of life.

However, if we look deeper there is a connection between Jesus' actions at Cana and his actions at Bethany, between the first and the seventh signs. In the first sign, a sign performed in the joy of life and love, Jesus asks, 'what do you want from me?'[11] In whatever manner and from whatever place we respond, at the heart of our reply will be a single word, and that word is 'life'. We want life. We respond in this way because, in so many ways, we allow ourselves to dwell in the darkness of the shadow of death. Here, in the seventh sign, Jesus responds to our answer with a simple command: 'then come out of the tomb!'

Sadly, it is not only in our hearts that we will find the signs of death. If we look, we will find them also in the sacramental symbol of life, the Church itself, and we cannot be blind to these signs, or hide them from the world and ourselves. To do so would be to ignore Jesus' command.

---

[11] John 2:4.

What, then, are the signs of death in the Church? The abuse of children by clergy, by the religious, or by any of those put in a position of responsibility by the Church, was and is a sign of death. The Church's slow response to this scandal, and its failure to reach out immediately to the victims of these abuses, was and is a sign of death. Equally, the failure of the Church to fully understand the reasons for such abuse and to make the necessary changes to ensure that the culture of clericalism which allowed for such abuse to take place is addressed, is a sign of death.[12]

These signs of death are an indication that, through inaction, we are allowing a part of the body of the Church to dwell in the tomb with Lazarus. That part of the Church that refuses to listen with an open and faithful heart to all of its people dwells in the tomb. That part of the Church that, knowingly or otherwise, oppresses parts of its body through a culture of triumphalism or inequality, dwells in the tomb. And that part of the Church that refuses an intimate encounter with the risen Jesus, through the sacraments, to those who live faithful and loving lives but who do not meet the strict norms of canon law, dwells in the tomb.

Yet this is not the will of God. Jesus calls to the Church, just as he called to Lazarus, to 'come out' of the tomb. The Church is called to be a sign of life for the world, to preach the gospel of life in pursuit of its fundamental

---

[12] See Most Rev. Diarmuid Martin, Archbishop of Dublin and Primate of Ireland, Address to International Dialogue on the Clergy Sexual Abuse Scandal at Marquette University, 4 April 2011. Archbishop Martin said, 'The culture of clericalism has to be analysed and addressed. Were there factors of clerical culture which somehow facilitated a disastrous abusive behaviour to continue for so long? Was it just through bad decisions by Bishops or superiors? Was there knowledge of behaviour which should have given rise to concern and which went unaddressed?'

'eschatological purpose'.[13] The Church must not find comfort by retreating into the darkness of the tomb. Instead, the Church must always find its home in the light of life. The Church, as the visible, sacramental and spiritual sign of God's love in this world, must always pursue her salvific mission to 'give shape in human history to the family of the son of God which will go on growing until our Lord's second coming'.[14]

The Church cannot allow itself to stand aloof above the world in some kind of spiritual security. It must be fully engaged in the activities of humankind, to give shape to our actions, to give shape to our life and to give shape to our encounters of love.

The Church has a mission which is salvific both in quality and in nature, in which she is tasked with reaching out to the whole of humanity. In so doing, she must preach the gospel of life which Jesus himself proclaimed. In short, her mission is to call to the world to 'come out' of the darkness of the cave of Lazarus's tomb and into the glorious light of the sons and daughters of God. Yet sadly, much of our world, many of the societies and communities in which we live, lie, like Lazarus, entombed in the darkness of death. A culture has increasingly developed through the latter part of the last century and the beginning of this century which unwittingly holds death at its heart. And, like the putrefying body of Lazarus, this culture spreads the evil and putrefying smell of death to each one of us.

What are these signs of death in the world? There are so many that it is hard to know where to begin. There is the

---

[13] *Gaudium et Spes*, 'On the Church in the Modern World':40 (Translation CTS 1966).
[14] Ibid.

grinding poverty in which billions of the world's poorest live. We have allowed ourselves in the developed world to become almost detached from this horror. Yet it is a sign of death when we worry about the effect of inflation on our take-home pay, or on our inability to afford a second holiday each year, or a better car, while millions of children in parts of Asia, Africa and South America scratch out a living by literally living off other people's rubbish, picking their way through HIV-infected needles, contaminated medical waste and human excrement in search of what few items can be resold. And for this they are paid no more than a few cents per day.

It is a sign of death when we fail to hold our politicians to account for spending more on weapons of death and destruction than on basic health care and education for our own young people, resulting in ever-increasing child poverty in our own cities. It is a sign of death when, even today, women and children are trafficked internationally, either for use as slave labour or for sex. It is a sign of death when we celebrate the resurrection of Christ at Easter with the gift of chocolate and the cocoa beans used to make that chocolate have been harvested by child labour in which the children suffer horrific injuries, risking decapitation, in order to harvest those beans.

These issues may seem too large to solve, too global in nature for us in our local communities to be involved with. Surely this is the job of the wider apostolic Church? However, the smell of death reaches out to and permeates our own communities too. By way of example, let us look at just one issue where the Church in the United Kingdom has yet to fully find her voice, that of the youth violence seen in so many of our cities today.

According to Tackling Knives Action Programme figures

provided by the Home Office,[15] in the ten police force areas measured in 2008,[16] there were over 2,850 incidents of sharp-instrument-related serious violence[17] involving those under the age of nineteen. In London alone in the same period, some 1,482 attacks took place involving those under nineteen. According to a Home Office report, almost 20,000 young people aged between thirteen and fifteen carry a knife for their own protection.[18] It is likely that many of the young people involved in these crimes come from families with a Christian heritage. If this is the case, then something must be going very wrong with the way that we pass on the experience of the Church to our sons and daughters. There must be something very wrong with how we are creating a safe spiritual space for them to grow and develop.

The Church rightly stresses the importance of the family unit in our society, but a Church which ignores and fails to act on the results of the breakdown of that unit is akin to a doctor preaching to a man about the dangers of unhealthy eating while ignoring the fact that he is in the midst of a heart attack. A Church which rightly preaches against the evils of abortion, but which at the same times ignores the evils of gang culture, knife and gun crime, is not taking a holistic approach to the gospel of life. Although it is, per-haps, easier to campaign for the rights of the unborn than it is to reach out to young people in the violence, distress and alienation of their lives, both signs of death must be addressed if the Church is to be faithful to her mission.

---

[15] http://www.homeoffce.gov.uk.
[16] Essex, Greater Manchester, Lancashire, Merseyside, Nottinghamshire, South Wales, Thames Valley, West Midlands, West Yorkshire and the Metropolitan Police Authority.
[17] This includes homicide, attempted murder, threats to kill, wounding, other wound-ing, GBH and ABH.
[18] Reported in the *Daily Telegraph*, 20 May 2011.

The Church in the United Kingdom has allowed herself to become characterised for many by issues of sexual ethics and morality. This is not only the fault of the media, indeed much has to do with the way that the Church engages with this media and finds her prophetic voice. For, in so doing, she has failed to grasp the holistic approach she must take to preaching the beauty of the gospel of life in all its facets.

It is easy to become desensitised to the painful reality of this issue when we are confronted by a sea of statistics. However, it is in the impact on the everyday lives of our neighbours that we can see the true pain. In the neighbourhood in which I live in South London, the threat of youth violence prevails on a daily basis. It seems no one is spared from its truly horrific effects. We have recently witnessed the latest victim of such crimes: Thusha, a five-year-old girl shot in the chest when a young man opened fire indiscriminately into a small newsagent shop. Thusha is believed to be the youngest victim of gun crime in London. It is in this reality that we see the signs of death and its effects. Thusha's mother, while waiting anxiously for her recovery, said:

> As a mother, I have deep love for all my children and what has happened to my daughter Thusha has left me feeling empty inside. I cannot eat or sleep properly until she opens her eyes. My daughter Thusha is such a sweet, quiet and helpful child, always smiling and laughing. I cannot wait to hear her voice again and hold her, [I] thank everyone who is praying for her ... I do not wish this to happen to another child.[19]

---

[19] Reported in the *Daily Telegraph*, 4 April 2011.

In the local community in which I and my family live, the Anglican community of St Anselm's became aware of the issue of knife and gun crime and how it was affecting many young people in the area. In response they began an outreach programme for the young people of their parish. However, it was only when one of St Anselm's altar servers was arrested and subsequently sentenced for the murder of a young man that the true horror of youth gangs and knife crime struck home, right to the very heart of the community. It was then that the community began to step up outreach programme in the much wider community, a programme that employs youth workers on a full-time basis and opens the doors and use of the church up to a variety of youth programmes for both the churched and the unchurched. The community is now seeking funds to convert half the worship space within the church into a restaurant, where young men and women, recently released from prison and on parole, can be taught new life skills and be given a job and a safe place to live in a welcoming parish. As Father Angus Aagaard, the community's parish rector, told me, 'When the knives came to our altar we knew we had to come out of the tomb.' Here, indeed, are signs of life in the darkness of the tomb; here are signs of resurrection.

The parents, family and friends of Jimmy Mizen are also signs of life and resurrection amidst the destruction of death. Jimmy was from a loving family of nine children. He enjoyed football, as an avid supporter of Millwall, and rugby, as a member of the local rugby club. He was also a faithful altar server at the Church of Our Lady of Lourdes in Lee. One Saturday afternoon, as Jimmy was celebrating his sixteenth birthday with his brother in a local bakery, he was confronted by a young man who challenged him to a fight. Jimmy refused, but the attacker smashed the bakery door, shattering the glass, and then attacked Jimmy with a piece of that glass, delivering a fatal blow to Jimmy's throat.[20]

Faced with the tragic loss of their son, one might have expected Jimmy's parents to be filled with justifiable anger, bitterness and even hatred. Yet this was not their response. Instead, publicly acknowledging that 'anger and confrontation are destroying our communities when most people just want a peaceful life',[21] Jimmy's family and friends have established the Jimmy Mizen Foundation. In addition to buying 'Jimmy buses' for use by local youth charities and organisations, the Foundation is devising a youth apprentice scheme and an awareness project. Jimmy's parents have also set up 'Families United', an organisation which brings together the families of the victims of youth knife and gun crime. Fittingly, the charity's motto is *e tenebris lux* – 'from the darkness comes light'.

The Church's teaching is not silent on these matters. The body of Catholic social teaching is impressive. However, teaching without physical action remains just that, teaching. In no way does it begin to give any real 'shape to human history' which the Church is mandated to do. The code of Catholic social teaching has often been described as 'the Catholic Church's best-kept secret'. Sadly this is true, but it should not be. The fault lies with us all, laity and clergy alike. Just as Jesus in the seventh sign intervened in death itself, we too, as the body of Christ, are

---

[20] Reported on BBC news, 11 May 2008.
[21] Barry Mizen, speaking shortly before the second anniversary of Jimmy's death, reported by BBC news, 10 May 2010.

called to intervene in the signs of death in our world and the signs of death in our local communities.

In assessing how we should respond, let us now turn to look at the actions of the central players in this drama: Martha, Mary, Lazarus and Jesus. As with all things, it is with Jesus that we should begin.

'I believe that you are the Christ, the Son of God'[22]

What is remarkable about the seventh sign is that through it we witness not only the divinity of Jesus in the execution of the sign, but – and this is of equal importance – also his very human side. In the previous six signs there has been little demonstration of emotion from Jesus. One could even argue that his approach in certain instances has been matter of fact. But here, in the seventh sign, John reveals to us a much more intimate side of Jesus. Jesus is portrayed as fully God, in the utter wonder and power of the sign, but also as fully man, in his compassion and love for Lazarus, Martha and Mary. At Bethany there is a passion to his actions. This is not the sign of a distant God working wonders, intervening in the lives of men from afar, but the sign of a God working a wonder precisely because he is God made man.

When the messenger is sent by Martha to tell Jesus that Lazarus is ill, his words are revealing: 'Lord, the man you love is ill.'[23] Unlike in the other healing signs at Cana, Bethesda and Siloam, Lazarus is not some stranger or mere acquaintance. He is loved by Jesus. Jesus refers to him as

---

[22] John 11:27.
[23] John 11:3.

'our friend'.[24] John goes out of his way, time and time again, to reinforce the message that Jesus is intimately connected, not only to this event, but also to the family of Lazarus. John narrates that 'Jesus loved Martha and her sister and Lazarus'.[25] Later, when Jesus meets Mary on the road, he becomes greatly distressed[26] at the sight of Mary's grief and the grief of the community who have come to mourn with her. In fact, Jesus is so disturbed by their anguish that he himself weeps.[27] Throughout the seventh sign, John makes no attempt to hide the humanity of Jesus, and Jesus himself makes no attempt to hide his own vulnerability. Thus we are reminded of the words of the Council Fathers: 'Whoever follows after Christ the perfect man, becomes himself more of a man.'[28] This is a theme we will return to later.

What is surprising, therefore, knowing as we do the deep emotional bond between Jesus and the family of Lazarus, is Jesus' response on first hearing the news of Lazarus's illness. Jesus does not rush to his friend's side. Rather he elects to stay where he is. There is no sense of urgency in his actions: 'when he heard that he was ill he stayed where he was for two more days'.[29] This is remarkable and seems to run counter to any claim of friendship or love Jesus had for Lazarus.

When we know that someone we love is in distress, we want to be with them, to be at their side. Indeed, in that context we have an innate and natural sense of urgency.

---

[24] John 11:11.
[25] John 11:5.
[26] John 11:33.
[27] John 11:35.
[28] *Gaudium et Spes*:41.
[29] John 11:6.

One Christmas, when my wife heard that her mother had been taken seriously ill and rushed to hospital for an emergency operation, she immediately left, in the middle of the night, to travel to Newcastle to be with her mother and family. She did not even have the opportunity to say goodbye to our young children. Quite properly, we reorganised our family life so that she could be with her father and sisters at a time of suffering and distress. This was the understandable and human reaction of a loving daughter to the news of her mother's pain.

However, Jesus does not seem to exhibit outwardly any sense of this urgency. Is John perhaps emphasising the true divinity of Jesus at the expense of his humanity? Jesus knows that Lazarus has died. He spells this out to the disciples later, when they assume that Lazarus is merely at rest, when he says bluntly, 'Lazarus is dead.'[30] If this were the case, then perhaps Jesus would be justified in taking his time to get to Bethany: Lazarus would be raised from the dead no matter when he got there. This could certainly be one possible explanation. However, it does not sit easily with the fact that Jesus loved not just Lazarus but also Martha and Mary. To delay his trip to Bethany without good reason would be at best insensitive and at worst callous in the context of his reaction to Lazarus's grieving sisters. Given Jesus' subsequent reaction upon seeing the grief of Mary and the mourners, it would also appear to be contradictory. Here, then, Jesus is not ignoring or denying his natural humanity, his natural desire to rush to the side of Lazarus and to comfort Mary and Martha, but rather he has to struggle to overcome such a desire for some greater purpose, some greater part of God's plan.

---

[30] John 11:14.

In addition, it was not only Jesus' desire to be with Martha and Mary that he had to struggle with, but also a natural and understandable fear. As we know, Bethany was extremely close to Jerusalem, probably less than a morning's walk. Jesus had left Jerusalem to travel to the far side of Jordan because, after a confrontation with the Jewish authorities in the temple,[31] the people there were threatening to stone him. There was a real and present danger to the life of Jesus which even the disciples recognised. When Jesus does elect to travel to Judea to see Martha and Mary, the disciples are alarmed: 'Rabbi, it is not long since the Jews were trying to stone you; are you going back there again?'[32]

Here, then, is a Jesus not in denial of his humanity but rather in total acceptance of it. Jesus struggles not only with his desire to reach out to the community at Bethany as soon as possible, but also with a natural fear for both himself and his disciples as to what awaits them at Judea. Yet Jesus, while not denying these very real emotions, sets them to one side. He overcomes them for a higher purpose, a greater good.

And what is this greater good? It is clear from John that this greater purpose is intrinsically linked to bringing the onlooking community at Bethany into a closer relationship with God the Father. Jesus' actions are designed to point the community towards his Father: 'it is for God's glory'.[33] And perhaps God's plan is why Jesus, attuned to the will of the Father, sacrifices his own natural and human desires for those of his Father. He sacrifices them so that, through the raising of Lazarus from the dead (rather than just

---

[31] John 8:59.
[32] John 11:8.
[33] John 11:4.

181

healing him before his death), those who witnessed the event would come to believe. In his prayer before calling Lazarus from the cave in which he has been entombed, Jesus says, 'Father I thank you for hearing my prayer. I myself knew that you hear me always, but I speak for the sake of all these who are standing around me, so that they may believe it was you who sent me.'[34]

In this final sign Jesus directs our gaze not to himself but to his Father, and it is through his action that we can come to know the Father better. The most important aspect of Jesus' action at Bethany is that he brings his humanity to the sign. This is not the sign of an aloof God, working miracles from afar. This is the sign of God made man, bringing the full force of his divinity and his humanity to overcome death itself. This is a sign performed by Jesus, 'the perfect man'. And so in undertaking the Church's salvific mission, we too must bring the full force of our compassionate humanity to the task – a humanity firmly empowered and enlivened by the divinity of Jesus; a humanity guided and inspired by the Holy Spirit in a threefold royal, prophetic and priestly ministry.

'Jesus loved Martha and her sister'[35]

Mary and Martha are very different in character from one another. From what we see in the story of the seventh sign and subsequently, when Jesus visits the family just before Passover, Mary can be described as the far more emotional sister. In the raising of Lazarus we see her falling at the feet

---

[34] John 11:41–42.
[35] John 11:5.

of Jesus in pain and anguish: she seems to rebuke Jesus for being late, saying that if only Jesus had come earlier then her brother Lazarus would not have died. Later we witness a different but equally emotive side when, after the raising of her brother, she falls again at the feet of Jesus – this time in order to anoint his feet with precious oils. There seems to be no middle ground with Mary. We witness moments of both physical anguish and physical joy.

This is not the case with Martha, who is portrayed in both events as being far more level-headed, more rational in her approach. In the seventh sign she walks out to meet Jesus alone. There is no demonstrable show of sadness; neither does she overtly plead for Jesus to raise Lazarus from the dead. Rather, her response is one of almost rational and accepting faith in Jesus and in the will of God. She declares to Jesus, 'but even now I know that God will grant whatever you ask of him.'[36] In this there is no demand, simply an acceptance that God's will be done rather than hers. Her words remind us of Mary's entreaty to Jesus in the first sign at Cana, 'They have no wine.'[37] Again, later, when Jesus visits Bethany, while Mary's response is to anoint Jesus' feet, wiping them with her hair, John tells us that Martha did not take centre stage; rather she 'waited on them'[38] as they ate dinner. Martha seems to lack the demonstrable passion of Mary. We can see in her, however, a thinking, faithful and purposeful person, focused on the task at hand.

Whether we empathise most with Mary or with Martha will depend on the sort of person we are. If we look around us in our families and in our communities, we will

---

[36] John 11:22.
[37] John 2:3.
[38] John 12:2.

recognise both Martha and Mary in the people we know, love and cherish. Most of us, if we are honest, will acknowledge an element of both Mary and Martha in each of us: the rational and the passionate, the thinking and the emotional. And we can be certain that in the context of the world today, at this particular moment in time, the Church needs to discover within herself the personality of both Mary and Martha if she is to fulfil her prophetic, eschatological role. The rational and the passionate are the two lungs of the Church and she must breathe deeply from both if she is to be healthy and call all to wholeness of life.

The Dominican priest Father Timothy Radcliffe OP, in his book *What's the Point of Being Christian?*,[39] characterises a growing divide in the Church as being like the divide between two political parties. On one side are the 'Communion Catholics' who see themselves 'primarily [as] members of the institution of the Church, the communion of believers'.[40] On the other side are the 'Kingdom Catholics' who see the Church as 'primarily the People of God on pilgrimage to the Kingdom of God'.[41] This divide seems to be an ever-growing one in which the protagonists both argue that only their style of Catholicism can or should survive within the Church. Their differences are becoming so strong that it is like trying to mix oil and water. However, as the Kentish poet Bill Hughes wryly observed, while oil and water do not mix, 'in a desert economy they had better learn to as both are essential'.[42]

Indeed, as Timothy Radcliffe has argued, the Church

---

[39] Timothy Radcliffe, *What's the Point of Being Christian?* (Burns and Oates, 2005).
[40] Ibid.
[41] Ibid.
[42] Bill Lewis, 'Conflict', taken from his collection *Communion* (Hangman Books, 1986).

cannot flourish without both parties.[43] So what can heal these divisions? Radcliffe writes that we must be drawn to a loyalty to the truth:

'For it is the truth that will set me free. It is in the truth that liberates that Kingdom and Communion Catholics can meet.[44]

At a more fundamental level, John Allen, the Vatican reporter for the *National Catholic Reporter*, suggests that we can no longer characterise Catholicism as having two sides – the left and the right. Rather, we now have tribal Catholicism, consisting of, for example, 'pro-life Catholics, peace and justice Catholics, liturgical traditionalist Catholics, neo-con Catholics, church-reform Catholics, feminist Catholics and so on'.[45] Allen goes on to argue that all these tribes must reach out a hand of friendship to one another. For it is only in the acceptance and easiness of friendship that they will rediscover each other's worth and value and each other's role in the Church's mission: 'Catholicism needs a grass-roots movement to rebuild zones of friendship in the church.'[46]

It is in the often forgotten truth of the Church's essential salvific and eschatological mission[47] that perhaps Kingdom and Communion Catholics and, indeed, all Catholic tribes will rediscover a freedom that will set them free. Tony Blair once quipped that his reform of the Labour Party would only be complete when the party learnt to love Peter Mandelson, who, for so many in the party, was seen

---

[43] Radcliffe, *What's the Point of Being Christian?*.
[44] Ibid.
[45] John L. Allen, 'Thoughts on post-tribal Catholicism', *National Catholic Reporter*, 15 April 2011.
[46] Ibid.
[47] *Gaudium et Spes*.

as the *bête noire* of New Labour. Perhaps the Church, too, will find a new maturity when all colours and tribes of Catholicism, Kingdom and Communion alike, not only learn to love one another in friendship but also realise how essential each is to the urgent and salvific mission of the Church.

'He called Lazarus out of the tomb'[48]

There would, of course, be no seventh sign without Lazarus. Indeed, it could be argued that not only is he central to the seventh sign, but he is also critical to the whole of the narrative and plot of the Gospel of John. It is because of Lazarus being called forth from the darkness and death of the tomb that Caiaphas convinces the Jewish authorities that Jesus must die.[49] Yet, while central to the sign and to the Gospel, he makes his appearance only in the final moments of the story. For much of the narrative he is hidden from view, in the darkness of the tomb. Nevertheless, we are left in no doubt of his presence throughout the events in Bethany. But what, though, do we know of Lazarus?

To begin with we know that Lazarus lives with his two sisters, which at that time would not have been uncommon. However, there is no mention of a wife or children and, perhaps from the fact that it is his sister Martha who waits at the table when Jesus visits Bethany, we can infer that he has neither a spouse nor his own offspring. What

---

[48] John 12:17.
[49] John 11:50.

we can be certain of is that Lazarus is loved. He is loved both in life and in death; he is loved by Jesus; he is loved by his sisters; and he is loved by the large crowd of mourners who come to wait with Mary and subsequently meet Jesus on the road to Bethany. In his life Lazarus was a sign of love. In his death he becomes much more. He becomes a sign of conversion.

Lazarus acts as a sign in both death and life. Following his raising, Lazarus becomes a sign of hope, a sign of expectation, a sign of the new Kingdom. Following the seventh sign the crowds gather at Jerusalem to welcome Jesus through the city gates because they have either witnessed the raising of Lazarus or have heard of the sign and now believe. In a very real sense, upon his resurrection Lazarus becomes a sign himself. He becomes a point of conversion.

However, for this to happen Lazarus *had to die.* Without his death he could not have been transformed; he could not have become a point of conversion for so many others. Both individually and as the community of the Church, we too are called to be a sign, to be a point of conversion for the world. And, like Lazarus, we too must die to our old selves and allow the power of the resurrection to transform us. The story of Lazarus is the story of change, of transformation and of new life. The story of Lazarus is the story of our baptism.

In the Italian city of Padua lies the Scrovegni Chapel. It is also known as the Arena Chapel because it was built on the site of a Roman arena. It is thought to have been built in the early fourteenth century and consecrated in 1305 as the private chapel of the Scrovegni family. The most remarkable features of the Arena Chapel are the thirty-seven frescoes painted on the interior walls by the Italian

Renaissance artist Giotto di Bondone.[50] These frescoes depict scenes from the life of Jesus. In one scene Giotto graphically depicts the raising of Lazarus. There is little romanticism in the painting. Lazarus is shown coming out of the tomb, still bound almost mummy-like by his burial garb. The part of Lazarus's face which is shown is pallid and grey, almost in a state of semi-decay, as if he were still going through a state of transformation. Indeed, the figures to the left of Lazarus have their mouths and noses covered to prevent them breathing in the decaying smell coming both from the tomb and from Lazarus himself. However, to the right of Lazarus is a follower of Jesus who has already removed his face covering and is reaching out to help the risen Lazarus. Mary and Martha, meanwhile, are seen at the feet of Jesus still imploring him to help. Giotto paints a scene of rapid transformation and action: while they are still pleading for their brother, Jesus has already acted.

Giotto's fresco is rich in symbolism and it can provide a rich and powerful allegory for us today as the Church and for the nature of our mission. Within the symbolism Lazarus represents humanity – a humanity which has in so many ways allowed itself to become mired in a culture and environment of death; a humanity which has become more comfortable decaying in the darkness of the tomb than being called out into the glorious light of God's love.

In the fresco, as in the Gospel, the followers of Jesus unbind Lazarus and in so doing they ignore the old law, for they touch what is still ritually unclean. By acting on Jesus'

---

[50] Giotto (1266–1337). Arguably Giotto's most famous and beautiful works can be found in the Basilica of St Francis in Assisi, depicting the life of St Francis, although there is argument as to the true provenance of this work. For a full description of Giotto's work at the Arena Chapel, see James H. Stubblebine (ed.), *Giotto: The Arena Chapel Frescoes* (W. W. Norton and Co., 1969); and John Ruskin, *Giotto and His Works in Padua* (Dodo Press, 2007).

command they accept the new law of the new covenant. They act as the agents of Lazarus's liberation from death and from the imprisonment and darkness of the tomb. We, too, as the followers of the risen Christ, must act as his agents of liberation, his agents of resurrection. Our urgent, primary and salvific mission is to unbind humanity from the captivity of death, to bring new life to those caught in the darkness of the tomb.

At the chapel in Padua the painting of Lazarus is directly above Giotto's depiction of the resurrection. This is no coincidence. There can be no resurrection without death, no new life without the pain of our mortality. This is our tear and our smile. For it is only in dying that we are born again to new life. As Bernadette Farrell writes in the hymn 'All That Is Hidden':

> If you would follow me, follow where life will lead
> Do not look for me among the dead
> For I am hidden in pain risen in love
> There is no harvest without sowing of grain.[51]

This is the challenge and the promise made to each of us and made real in our baptism. This is the promise that the Church must offer to the world as we echo the words of Jesus, with many voices but one heart, 'Come out of the tomb, come out!'

---

[51] Bernadette Farrell, 'All That Is Hidden', in *Restless is the Heart* (Oregon Catholic Press, 2006)

Our Journey's End

We have nearly come to the end of our journey with the beloved disciple. In and through the signs we have found Jesus calling us to his promise and challenging us to action. Although the signs are given that we might believe, they are also given that we might act. If we are to allow the signs to have relevance to us today, we must allow the Gospel of John to have a transformative effect on us. We must allow the words and actions of Jesus to change us from within, so that we too, like Lazarus, become visible signs of that same promise and challenge of Jesus for all those whom we encounter. In short, we are called to be truly sacramental to one another. The power of the Holy Spirit, working in and through us, has the power not only to change us individually, but also, through that very change, to transform the communities in which we live and worship. If we are truly to live and become visible signs, this is not the end of our journey but the beginning.

How, then, do we live the signs in our communities? How would a parish community act in truly living and witnessing to the signs in its ministry? How would its royal, prophetic and priestly ministry be shaped if it fully embraced the challenge and the promise given by Jesus through the signs? How would the people of that community live their lives? Let us for a moment imagine. Let us pay a visit to the parish community of St Mary's.

St Mary's is an inner-city church. It has a rich and widely diverse cultural and social make-up. There are members of the parish whose families have lived in that part of town for generations. Indeed, some families have been coming to St Mary's for more than three or four generations, through peacetime and through war. However, times are changing. There is now a large migrant community living within the parish boundaries. Here can be found first- and second-generation arrivals from Africa, the Caribbean, South America and Eastern Europe. This has inevitably led to some tensions between the new communities arriving in the area and those which have been established there for many years.

Economically, too, the community is diverse. It includes young single and married professionals who live in the newly renovated warehouses and constructed apartments by the old docks adjacent to the parish. Most have chosen to live in the area because of its proximity to the City's financial district where they work. This community comprises lawyers, accountants, bankers and City professionals. Their lives are busy, and although financially they are all more than comfortable, they are all poor when it comes to the time that they have available outside work.

On the other side of the community are huge swathes of social housing where the economic outlook is far bleaker. Some families living there have become dependent on one breadwinner, and the principal earner perhaps has two jobs, on or just above the minimum salary, in order to pay for the basic costs of keeping their young family above the waterline. Some families have single-parents who rely heavily on the state for support. There are also families who have become generationally dependent upon state benefits and support, where both parents and children fall into the category of the long-term unemployed.

In addition there is a growing number of the newly unemployed, residents who have, due to government cutbacks, recently lost their jobs in the public sector or construction trade. More worryingly, the number of single unemployed persons under the age of twenty-five is rapidly increasing. Indeed, the borough in which St Mary's is situated has one of the highest averages of youth unemployment in the country. Recent reports show that crime is also increasing. Many of the older residents in the community are too afraid to leave their homes in the evening for fear of falling victim to crime.

Moreover, due to government financial restrictions many of the borough-wide programmes aimed at young people have had drastic reductions made to their already small budgets. Youth clubs and library services are suffering and many facilities have either already had to shut or will soon do so.

How, then, has St Mary's responded to the challenges of ministry in this very mixed community? First and foremost, all activity at St Mary's finds its basis, its reason for being and its rationale through and in the celebration of the Eucharist. The parish priest, Father Patrick, realised on his arrival that if the parish was to thrive and have a positive impact on the wider community, all of its activities must find their centre in an intimate and sacramental encounter with Jesus. However, he also realised that this encounter had to be vibrant and life-giving. This central celebration of community had to be just that: true and alive.

One of the first things Patrick did on arrival in the parish, realising his own limitations both of time and of voice, was to take a leap of faith. He employed a full-time musician and liturgist to help lead the community in prayerful worship. At the time he did this, he was not at all sure how the parish would be able to afford what others might describe as a luxury. Mass attendance in the years before his arrival had fallen to just over one hundred. And, during Holy Week for example, few of his parishioners would come to any of the Triduum celebrations.

Nevertheless, he engaged Julie as the parish liturgist. Together they set about establishing a choir made up of both children and adults. At first, many in the parish were reluctant to join, but gradually they began to enjoy coming together in community to sing and praise God in each other's fellowship. To begin with the choir was a small group numbering some ten people. However, as people were attracted by the directness, relevance and vibrancy of Patrick's preaching, as well as by the prayerfulness and diversity of music within the liturgy, both the congregation in general and the choir slowly began to grow.

At the same time Patrick brought together a group of parishioners to help him plan and organise the liturgies. He ensured that every element of the community was represented so that he could be sure that the celebration of the Eucharist would speak to all members of the parish, no matter what their status or background.

Now, some four years later, there are over forty members of the choir and Mass attendance exceeds six hundred people on any given Sunday. The liturgy at St Mary's has become the focal point of celebration within the community; it attracts new members to the parish each week. Many Catholics who had lapsed in their practice have begun to return to the Church, attracted by the genuine feeling of companionship and love within the parish and by the beauty and celebration of the liturgy. At the sign of peace, people use each other's names and even dare to cross the aisle to shake each other's hands warmly. Patrick is proud to relate that, on one such occasion, two of his parishioners met each other for the first time and, shortly after, were married in the parish. Since then the couple's three children have all been baptised at St Mary's, which for the entire family has become a place to celebrate not only their community but also their lives together as a family.

Patrick also persuaded some of the young professionals living in the area to read at Mass every Sunday. Proclamation of the Word of God began to be seen as important ministry within the parish rather than just something that would be done by whoever was unlucky enough not to avoid the parish priest's eye on Sunday morning. Patrick gathered the group together for a retreat to start their ministry, and now that original group and subsequent readers meet one evening a month to read and pray the Scriptures together, a process during which they have forged new friendships by breaking open the Word of God and sharing, quite literally, the wine of fellowship.

Realising how many young families lived in the community, Patrick also instigated the first Sunday of each month as a children's liturgy. Young families began to come to this Mass, attracted by the music and a service which was aimed at their children and where they felt that they would not be reprimanded if their children were not, at times, the best behaved. The Sunday liturgy for children is now led by a group of young mothers. Catherine, a mother whose family has lived in the parish for generations, leads the group. She is also the safeguarding officer, whose job is focused on child protection for the parish, a role that she and the community take very seriously.

As the congregation began to grow, particularly through listening to the Word of God from the lectern and being fed from the table of the Eucharist, people within the community began to be inspired to work together for the good of the parish community as well as for the wider community. This has taken many different forms and the actions have become contagious.

To begin with, Catherine and some of the other mothers realised that during the long summer holidays many parents were put under extra pressure. There was very little for their young children to do and, with local government library and playgroup closures and family budgets becoming increasingly stretched, many of the children were being neglected. Accordingly, they started Rainbow Week, which takes place every July. All children under the age of seven are welcome to attend and there is no cost, although people are invited to make whatever contributions they are able to afford. During Rainbow Week the children are taught to play creatively with each other, through a lively mixture of song, dance, acting and art. On at least one of the days the parish subsidises a day out in the country for all the children. Rainbow Week ends with the 'Mass of Colour' in which the children celebrate the diversity of being together in community.

On each day throughout the year there is a morning Mass at St Mary's. Patrick is always surprised and happy to see at least forty or so parishioners attend this service. The service lasts around twenty-five minutes, but each day a group of at least twenty parishioners stay behind to pray together. Much of this prayer is spontaneous. Sometimes someone will start reciting the rosary. On other occasions a person will start by praying aloud. Sometimes the group just sits in attentive and listening silence. Always, however, the group prays together each day for twenty or so minutes for the needs of the community as expressed by Patrick on the previous Sunday. There is now also a prayer board, where parishioners have started to leave prayer requests for the weekday group.

Five of the parishioners, Joseph, Malcolm, Harry, Sharon and Eva, have stood for and been elected as local councillors. They come from different political backgrounds and parties, yet once every three months they come together as a group with members of the parish community to discuss and pray together, to see how they can work as Christians across party political lines to give voice to their faith in the wider community.

Eva's daughter, Denise, was excluded from school at the age of thirteen. She had a tough upbringing, arriving in this country from Africa when she was five, and had always found it difficult to study in a language which was not her first. Sadly, she was not given the teaching attention she required and her boredom soon turned to disruptive behaviour. However, on being excluded she was sent to a borough day centre for lessons. There, Denise met many similar young people who had also been pushed out to the margins. Together they found a community in which they could find acceptance, and a connection with each other through belonging to a gang.

Denise's life reached a turning point when one of her closest friends was murdered in a knife fight between rival gangs. He was just fourteen. It was then that Denise realised that she could either follow a similar road or try to do something different. With the parish's help she started her own anti-knife campaign. It started in a small way with

Denise printing and selling T-shirts and organising a disco to raise awareness. However, it has gone from strength to strength and she has now recruited a team of ten ex-gang members who visit local schools and talk to young people about the dangers of knife crime and gang violence. The group hosts a meeting every week in the church community hall. Through their example and engagement, Patrick has persuaded one of the parish community, the owner of a local business, to sponsor a full-time youth worker to be employed by the parish on an initial three-year basis. Six of the young people have started to do voluntary work in the parish. One of the first tasks they have undertaken is to accompany some of the more elderly members of the community to and from evening services or meetings, so that they can come to the community in safety and without fear.

John and Vicky, too, are now regular attendees at Mass on Sunday. Both are teachers and work in a multicultural and religiously mixed school in the borough. Working with young people of different faiths and none, they have come to realise that there is much that the diverse faith groups within the community can learn from each other. They initially reached out to Father Kevin, who is the local Anglican vicar. Patrick and he were introduced and both realised quickly that they had much more in common than they had thought. John, Vicky, Patrick and Kevin have now started a group which meets every two months and its members include parishioners from St Mary's and St Barnabas, the Anglican community. At each meeting the group comes together to celebrate their common Christian heritage, but also to share a simple meal in which they can come to know each other and their respective traditions better. Through these simple meals, friendships have been formed across the divide. In addition, once a year each parish plays host to the other for an ecumenical service based upon the fellowship and community that have already been built. They have also begun discussions with the local Baptist church about taking part during the next year.

Sarah and Peter, another young couple from the community, have just returned from working abroad. They both work for a large international bank and were offered a two-year placement in South Africa. Having no real ties or commitments in England, they jumped at the chance. Now, having witnessed the poverty which exists in that country, they have returned and are spearheading a project which is linking St Mary's to the parish church of Christ the King in the Alexandra Township in Johannesburg. The project is still at an early stage, but it is hoped it will initially involve the community at St Mary's sponsoring a much-needed educational project in the township. Betty, one of the older parishioners at St Mary's, has been inspired by Sarah's and Peter's commitment. She has started to reflect on some of the choices she has made in her life, and has started a free trade stall at the church. Each Sunday she is overwhelmed by the generosity of the parishioners and is always running out of stock.

Frank has been coming to St Mary's now for three years. He left the diocesan priesthood over five years ago and it took him two years to find a parish where he felt truly welcomed and not judged. When Patrick saw him at Mass one Sunday, he was both overjoyed and quick to ensure that Frank's talents within the community would not be wasted. Frank now leads a team of four catechists who all work together to welcome adults into the Church through the Journey in Faith programme. Three of these catechists also took part in the programme themselves as part of their own journeys in faith. Last Easter, at the Vigil Mass, eleven adults were received joyfully into full communion with the Church.

Jonathan is a lawyer who works in the centre of the City's financial district. He has been coming to St Mary's for over ten years and has seen many changes both in the parish community and in the wider area. Lately he has become increasingly concerned at the number of young people in the community who are unemployed. He and others have begun a mentoring scheme for young unemployed people. Eight members of the parish have each undertaken to mentor two young unemployed members of the community. They meet with them once every two weeks to provide guidance on CV-writing, job applications and interview techniques. Jonathan has also engaged both a number of local businesses and others in the City to offer work placements to these young people in order to help them gain the experience they require. The project, named after the parish community, has become so successful that the Anglican church at St Barnabas has decided to start its own scheme, which will work in conjunction with the St Mary's project.

Patrick has been concerned for some time that, as a result of the economic crisis, the number of parishioners who are starting to struggle financially has increased. As a result, after consulting the entire parish, he has started to set aside ten per cent of the Sunday collection for a fund to help any member of the parish who may need financial help. At first, Patrick was worried that in so doing the parish might begin to struggle financially. However, he was amazed that, after explaining what was proposed to the parish, the weekly collection actually went up by twenty per cent. With the additional money Patrick has also been able to add much-needed funds to some of the other parish projects.

Underpinning all these activities, the highlight of the parish year is at the beginning of Lent when the week-long parish retreat takes place. During the retreat, nightly services are held centred around the Word of God. Members of the parish come together to listen and to seek direction as to what the Spirit of God is calling them to do, both individually and together, as a community. It is a time of reflection and a time of hope. During Holy Week, after the ultimate act of service, that of the washing of the feet at the celebration of Holy Thursday, the parish collectively and with one voice renews its promise of service. That promise is one of service to each other, to the local community and to the wider Church. Together they pray:

Heavenly Father

We thank you for bringing us together as community in St Mary's. We thank you for the example you have given us through your Son, to bend low, like him, and wash the feet of our neighbours in service. We promise, Father, nourished at the table of your Eucharist and inspired by your Word, that during the coming year we shall together live out the royal, priestly and prophetic mission that you have called us to through the waters of our baptism. And we promise, in that mission to:

— reach out to the poor, to the homeless, to the alone, both here and in communities throughout the world, and in so doing give generously of our time and resources and our love, and to also speak out against injustice wherever we see it;

— reach out to our young people, that they may find in this community a place where they can grow safely and be gently guided in their search for the truth;

— reach out with a listening and open heart in a spirit of faith and doubt, to all people of faith and of none. To build bridges with our Christian brothers and sisters, that together through the fellowship of love and community all will see a living testament to your Gospel;

— reach out and support each other, in our happiness and in our sorrows, in our joys and in our sadness. We promise to be a people of prayer always listening for your still small voice calling and challenging us.

We make this prayer through your Son Jesus, with and in whom we live and find our being. Amen.

All who look in at the parish of St Mary's are truly amazed, not only by the sense of life and vibrancy that is shared, but also by the deep experience of familial love upon which the community is built.

You may think that living the community life of St Mary's is the impossible dream. Surely, you may say, this could not happen in my parish community? Yet all of these activities, and more, are happening within various Christian communities in South London. Inspired by the Word of God and fed at his Eucharistic table, people are living their faith in action and in so doing are partaking in the joy and celebration of community to which Jesus calls us. For John has given us the signs not only that we might believe, but, in believing, that we might also act.

On our journey, John has taken us from the joy and celebration of community and love at Cana to the joyous hope of resurrection through Jesus at Bethany. We can be sure that, like the royal official, we will have moments of doubt on the journey, and that, like the blind young man, our faith will be tested in the fires and heat of the furnace of opposition. However, the message that is central to the meaning of the signs is that through them Jesus calls us to live out our Christian mission of love and service today; to reach out to the alienated and lost in our society like the sick man at Bethesda. Yet we can be certain, too, that on our journey we will encounter the risen life-giving and liberating Lord, through both Sacrament and Word, and through the intimate sacramental sign of the risen Christ living within each of our brothers and sisters whom we encounter in each moment of our lives.

And so, as we draw to the end of this book, we are reminded of the words of the blessed disciple himself: 'There were many other signs that Jesus worked in the sight of the disciples, but they are not recorded in this book. These are recorded so that you may believe that Jesus is the Christ, the Son of God, and that believing this you may have life through his name.'[52]

As we journey on in our lives, in the communities in which we live, work and worship, let us live our lives as signs of love. Let us live our lives as signs of hope. Let us live our lives as signs of resurrection. But, most importantly, let us live our lives in the sure and certain knowledge that he who has called us each by name, through the waters of our baptism, walks with us on each step of our journey; and that he will continue to do so until that day when we shall see and meet him in the fullness of his glory and the wonder of his all-accepting and forgiving love.

[52] John 20:30-31.

Bibliography

The New Jerusalem Bible (Darton, Longman & Todd, 1985)

Vatican texts:

Centesimus Annus

Lumen Gentium

Gaudium et Spes

Verbum Domini

Salvific Doloris

Bauckham, Richard, *The Testimony of the Beloved Disciple* (Baker Academic, 2007).
Benedict XVI, Homily given at the Mass of the Lord's Supper on Holy Thursday, 5 April 2007, at the Basilica of St John Lateran.
Benedict XVI, Homily given at the Mass and Eucharistic Procession on the Solemnity of Corpus Domini, 26 May 2005, in the square in front of the Basilica of St John Lateran.
Brown, Raymond E., *The Gospel and Epistles of John, A Concise Commentary*, 4th ed. (Liturgical Press, 1992)

Dear, John, *The Life and Example of Jean Donovan* (CommonDreams.org., 2005).

Evans, Craig A., *Jesus and the Ossuaries: What Burial Practices Reveal about the Beginning of Christianity* (Baylor University Press, 2003).

Gibran, Khalil, *A Tear and a Smile* (1914).

Graffy, Adrian, *Alive and Active, The Old Testament beyond 2000* (Columbia Press, 1999).

Hahn, Scott, *Letter and Spirit* (Doubleday, 2005).

Hahn, Scott, *The Lamb's Supper* (Doubleday, 1998).

Hughes, Gerard W., *God in all Things* (Hodder and Stoughton, 2003).

Hughes, Gerard W., *God, Where are You?* (Darton, Longman & Todd, 1997).

Hughes, Gerard W., *In Search of a Way* (Darton, Longman & Todd, 1986).

Jamison, Dom Christopher, *Sanctuary – Monastic Steps for Everyday Living* (Orion Books, 2006).

John Paul II, Homily on the occasion of his inauguration to the pontificate (22 October, 1978).

Kavanaugh, Kieran and Otilio Rodriguez (trans.), *The Collected Works of St John of the Cross* (ISP Publications, 1991).

Kolodiejchuk, Brian (ed.), *Mother Teresa Come Be My Light* (Rider, 2008).

Lewis, Bill, *Communion* (Hangman Books, 1986).

Méndez Montoya, Angel F., *The Theology of Food Eating and the Eucharist* (Wiley Blackwell, 2009).

Nazir-Ali, Bishop Michael, 'Extremism Flourished as UK Lost Christianity, *Daily Telegraph*, 11 January 2008.

Nichols, Archbishop Vincent, Homily given on the date of his installation at Westminster Cathedral, 21 May 2009.

Obama, Barack, *Audacity of Hope* (Canongate Books, 2007).

Peck, M. Scott, *The Road Less Travelled* (Arrow Books, 1990).

Radcliffe, Timothy, *What's the Point of Being Christian?* (Burns and Oates, 2005).

Radcliffe, Timothy, *Why Go to Church?* (Continuum, 2008).

Ruskin, John, *Giotto and His Works in Padua* (Dodo Press, 2007).

Schroeder, Robert G., *John Paul II and the Meaning of Suffering – Lessons from a Spiritual Master* (Our Sunday Visitor, 2008).

Shanley, John Patrick, *Doubt – A Parable* (Theatre Communications Group, 2005).

Thérèse of Lisieux, *Story of a Soul: The Autobiography of St Thérèse of Lisieux* (Christian Classics Ethereal Library, ccel.org).

Stubblebine, James (ed.), *Giotto: The Arena Chapel Frescoes* (W. W. Norton and Co., 1965).

Vanier, Jean, *Drawn into the Mystery of Jesus through the Gospel of John* (Darton, Longman & Todd, 2004).

Williams, Rowan, *Silence and Honey Cakes: The Wisdom of the Desert* (Lion Hudson, 2003).

Wylen, Stephen M., *The Jews in the Time of Jesus* (Paulist Press, 1994).